THE CINEMA OF
OUSMANE SEMBENE

**Recent Titles in
Contributions in Afro-American and African Studies**
Series Advisers: John W. Blassingame and Henry Louis Gates, Jr.

The Afro-Yankees: Providence's Black Community in the Antebellum Era
Robert J. Cottrol

A Case of Black and White: Northern Volunteers and the Southern Freedom Summers, 1964–1965
Mary Aickin Rothschild

Gatekeepers of Black Culture: Black-Owned Book Publishing in the United States, 1817–1981
Donald Franklin Joyce

The Craft of an Absolute Winner: Characterization and Narratology in the Novels of Machado de Assis
Maria Luisa Nunes

Black Marriage and Family Therapy
Constance E. Obudho, editor

The Womb of Space: The Cross-Cultural Imagination
Wilson Harris

Dark Continent: Africa as Seen by Americans
Michael McCarthy

The Black Press in the South, 1865–1979
Henry Lewis Suggs, editor

Voices from Under: Black Narrative in Latin America and the Caribbean
William Luis, editor

Contemporary Public Policy Perspective and Black Americans: Issues in an Era of Retrenchment Politics
Mitchell F. Rice and Woodrow Jones, Jr., editors

Student Culture and Activism in Black South African Universities: The Roots of Resistance
Mokubung O. Nkomo

THE CINEMA OF OUSMANE SEMBENE,
A Pioneer of African Film

FRANÇOISE PFAFF

Foreword by
Thomas Cripps

Contributions in Afro-American and African Studies, Number 79

Greenwood Press
Westport, Connecticut · London, England

Library of Congress Cataloging in Publication Data

Pfaff, Francoise.
 The cinema of Ousmane Sembene, a pioneer of African film.

 (Contributions in Afro-American and African studies, ISSN 0069-9624; no. 79)
 Bibliography: p.
 Includes index.
  1. Sembene, Ousmane, 1923–   . 2. Moving-picture producers and directors—Senegal—Biography. I. Title. II. Series.
 PN1998.A3S4256   1984   791.43′0233′0924   84-3842
 ISBN 0-313-24400-6 (lib. bdg.)

Copyright © 1984 by Françoise Pfaff

All rights reserved. No portion of this book may be reproduced, by any process or technique, without the express written consent of the publisher.

Library of Congress Catalog Card Number: 84-3842
ISBN: 0-313-24400-6
ISSN: 0069-9624

First published in 1984

Greenwood Press
A division of Congressional Information Service, Inc.
88 Post Road West
Westport, Connecticut 06881

Printed in the United States of America

10 9 8 7 6 5 4 3 2 1

A Hélène et Louise Pfaff,
ma mère et ma grand-mère

CONTENTS

Illustrations	ix
Foreword	xi
Preface	xv
Acknowledgments	xix

Part 1

1. Background to the Cinema of Ousmane Sembene 3
2. Sembene, a Griot of Modern Times 29
3. The Africanness of Sembene's Film Language 43

Part 2

4. *Borom Sarret* (1963): One Day in the Life of a Dakar Cartman 99
5. *Black Girl* (1966): From Book to Film 113
6. *Mandabi* (1968): Illiteracy versus Bureaucracy 127
7. *Emitai* (1971): Myths, Traditions, and Colonialism 141
8. *Xala* (1974): Realism and Symbolism 149

9. *Ceddo* (1976): A Story of the Past with
   Contemporary Significance — 165
10. Conclusion — 179

Appendix 1 Sembene: A Biographical Sketch — 181

Appendix 2 Sembene's Films: Credits — 185

Appendix 3 Sembene's Impact on Filmmaking — 191

Bibliography — 197

Index — 201

ILLUSTRATIONS

Following page 83
1. *Black Girl,* 1966
2. *Borom Sarret,* 1963
3. *Borom Sarret,* 1963
4. *Mandabi,* 1968
5. *Emitai,* 1971
6. *Emitai,* 1971
7. *Emitai,* 1971
8. *Xala,* 1974
9. *Xala,* 1974
10. *Xala,* production still
11. *Ceddo,* 1976
12. *Ceddo,* production still
13. *Ceddo,* 1976
14. *Ceddo,* 1976

FOREWORD

In the past two decades, the films of Ousmane Sembene have risen in the eyes of the world's critics from mere African curiosities to metaphors whose universality crosses cultural boundaries. In the beginning at Cannes in 1966, his *Black Girl* seemed no more than "a budding film consciousness . . . that may be heard from." And for a time, critics seemed to praise him mainly for making "no concessions to the expectations and desires of western audiences." But as early as 1970, the mass-circulation *Newsweek* found his work "momentously beautiful" and carped at "the nitwits who distribute most commercial movies in the United States" for their blindness to his talents.

As Sembene's audience broadened, critics found increasing evidence that he spoke directly to them and their constituencies. To an American critic, Sembene's *Mandabi* seemed "a staple of all cultures" and echoed a theme from Mark Twain's *The Million Pound Note*. A West Coast critic, upon seeing the same film, concluded that "human nature in Senegal is rather like human nature in San Francisco." And in London, the critic of the *Financial Times* found his comedy strikingly "Jonsonian."

Soon, the world's established film institutes celebrated his achievements. The National Film Theatre in London played his work on more than one occasion. The American Film Institute gave him several evenings in the form of both screenings and scholarly lectures by visiting critics. The Enoch Pratt Free Library in Baltimore bought four of his films for free distribution to its mainly black clientele. And the Museum of Modern Art offered a season of fifteen years of Senegalese cinema.

And yet this flow of critical acclaim has not been accompanied by a canon of thorough scholarly analysis. In fact, the literature on Ousmane Sembene is painfully thin, inaccessible to English and American readers, and often impenetrably political in texture. Yet of all contemporary African filmmakers, Sembene remains the most inviting to inquiry by outsiders. At the risk of seeming parochially European, we might label him a "Renaissance man" in the sense that he has lived enough variety of experience for several ordinary lives. He has been a longshoreman in Marseilles, a soldier in the French Army, a student of film in Moscow, a world traveler, a novelist, and an African divided by an urge to live in traditional Wolof society while hectoring the Western, urbanized, detribalized class that rules his native Senegal. Unfortunately, he and his films have not attracted English-speaking critics of equal range, capable of examining the art of the cinema across cultural lines drawn by tribalism, colonialism, and Marxism. Until now.

I first met Françoise Pfaff several years ago, while she was writing her doctoral dissertation at the University of Paris on a topic in which we shared an interest—blacks in American movies. Since that time, almost a decade ago, I have seen several versions of this critical essay on Sembene and have watched it grow into a solid, innovative inquiry into the work of Africa's most artistically, culturally, and politically interesting filmmaker.

This accomplishment has been no easy matter. In essence, Pfaff has approached Sembene through their shared culture—French—and has attempted by means of it to penetrate Sembene's Africanness. With good effect, she has applied Sembene's own sense of the place of the *griot*—the tribal storyteller—to her critical method. At the same time, she has called our attention to the use of the artifacts and masks of African traditional life that are imbedded in the text of Sembene's work. And like Sembene, she has examined the tension between the traditional and the modern in African life. Finally, she has taken the trouble to master the arcane system of motion picture financing, production, and distribution that is a fossil of the colonial order into which Sembene had been born.

Thus, the reader will find in this study of Sembene's films a coherence derived from understanding the delicate balance of forces at work in African society—European and African, French and Wolof, urban and rural, modern and traditional. That is to say, Pfaff uses the very tensions that animate and color Sembene's own films as modes of critical inquiry.

In sum, *The Cinema of Ousmane Sembene, A Pioneer of African Film* provides a densely packed, almost anthropological introduction to the work of an important filmmaker whose films have cried out for a serious, book-length, critical examination.

Thomas Cripps

PREFACE

For many years the media, especially the cinema, essentially emphasized the exotic and isolated strangeness of Africa within a seemingly immutable framework, while the authenticity and changes in the life of its peoples were frequently neglected or disregarded. Western cinema was largely responsible for such a misrepresentation. Consequently, many non-Africans saw the "dark continent" as a static land of mystery whose issues and aspirations, seen in a global perspective, were either unknown or misunderstood. The lack of knowledge of the customs and concerns of the peoples of Africa was in sharp contrast to the growing importance of that continent in foreign relations.

The 1960s were years of drastic change in many of the countries of Africa which had gained their independence after a century or more of European colonial tutelage. These newly acquired freedoms, bringing about a new self-awareness and assertiveness, stimulated the expression of the people, particularly those working in the arts. A new breed of artists emerged, the African-born filmmakers who were to convey to the world a more authentic and realistic portrayal of Africa from an African viewpoint.

Ousmane Sembene of Senegal, the first and most successful of these African filmmakers, is considered the pioneer of African film. His productions are highly representative of some of the trends of the recently emerged sub-Saharan African cinema. It was after achieving prominence as a writer that Sembene turned to filmmaking. His purpose was to address effectively all of his compatriots, many of whom are still illiterate.

Sembene's films have been internationally recognized as reflectors of and vehicles for African cultures. Although his works are widely appreciated by selected audiences especially interested in African affairs or film, they are often ignored by the general non-African public. The primary purpose of this book is to familiarize the public at large with the cinema of Ousmane Sembene. It also intends to compensate for the absence of any detailed analysis of Sembene's films released in the English language. To this date, only Paulin Soumanou Vieyra's *Sembène Ousmane Cinéaste* (1972), describing the early part of the Senegalese director's career, is available in French for viewers eager to become better acquainted with Africa through the motion pictures of its most significant filmmaker. Thus, the need for an in-depth study of Sembene's films has become more and more apparent.

The present work stems from ideas generated over a ten-year period through personal encounters with Ousmane Sembene, both in Africa and the United States; the writing of articles and conference papers; the teaching of film-related courses; and a number of animated discussions with colleagues and friends. The basic structure of this study derives from a concern to show why Sembene should be considered a pioneer of African film. If, indeed, Ousmane Sembene provides the inspiration for a truly African cinema, establishing new bridges between film and the African reality, it is important to determine what previous images of black Africa dominated the screen before he took hold of a camera. It is necessary as well to describe the sociocultural, political, and economic context in which African film appeared, namely Francophone African cinema, of which Sembene is the leading figure. A subsequent analysis identifies, documents, and discusses the aesthetics, sociopolitical, and metaphorical value of Sembene's cinema within an African frame of reference rather than solely according to limiting and sometimes ill-adapted Western theories of film criticism.

Although stressing the stylistic and technical characteristics of Sembene's films, this book focuses on their content at a realistic and symbolic level. Thus, in the following interpretive study of the director's most significant motion pictures, the theme most reflective of Sembene's creative eclecticism is chosen for each film rather than, necessarily, the primary theme of each film, although they do in many instances coincide.

Finally, my perception of Sembene's moving pictures is by no means exhaustive, and other interpretations can be equally justified. My only hope is to open the way to further studies of Ousmane Sembene's film contribution to the enrichment of man's intercultural heritage.

ACKNOWLEDGMENTS

My deepest gratitude is extended to: Ousmane and Carrie Sembene for their help through the years; Howard University, whose Faculty Research Grant and Andrew W. Mellon Fund provided financial support at various stages of this work; Thomas Cripps, for his thorough reading and invaluable advice; Laura P. Carson, Andrew Crockett and James H. Kennedy for their meticulous proofreading; Abiyi Ford for his continuous support; Mbye B. Cham, Martha K. Cobb, Marjorie Crockett, Annette Ivory Dunzo, Haile Gerima, Maurice A. Lubin, Mildred Hill-Lubin, Luce de Vitry Maubrey, Regis Maubrey, Keith Q. Warner, and Lillian S. Williams for their critique of the first draft of the manuscript; Mamadou Diagne for his assistance in the translation of Wolof; Cheikh Ngaido Bah, Georges Caristan, Souleymane Cissé, Yves Diagne, Maguette Diop, Abdou Fary Faye, Med Hondo, Niagane, Samba S. Sakho, Ababacar Samb, Momar Thiam, Mahama Johnson Traoré, and Paulin Soumanou Vieyra, who responded enthusiastically to my interviews; the staff of the Library of Congress and, in particular, Laverne Page of the African and Middle Eastern Division, and Barbara Humphrys, Patrick Sheehan, and Emily Sieger of the Motion Picture, Broadcasting, and Recorded Sound Division, who greatly facilitated my research; the librarians of the British Film Institute in London, the Museum

Acknowledgments

of Modern Art in New York, and the Institut des Hautes Etudes Cinématographiques in Paris; and to Claire Méhat, for her secretarial skills and patience in deciphering my handwriting. Finally, I would like to express my thanks to Maureen Melino and James T. Sabin of Greenwood Press, whose interest and guidance gave me the necessary incentive to pursue this work to its completion.

PART 1

1
BACKGROUND TO THE CINEMA OF OUSMANE SEMBENE

> Before we started to make films, Europeans had shot films about the African continent. Most of the Africans we saw in those films were unable to set one foot in front of another by themselves. African landscapes were used as settings. Those films were based on European stories.[1]

This remark by Sembene describes the overall picture of Africa provided by Western cinema in an era when the African continent was under European domination. For many years, Western films bestowed the world with a paternalistic and superficial view of Africa, a view which was reinforced by the news media and popular literature. Those films were generally aimed at a non-African public and, with a few exceptions, condoned and even justified Western colonialism in Africa.

The cinema of Ousmane Sembene illustrates African reality from an African perspective. Consequently, it presents images which are drastically different from the "Tarzanistic" pictures of Africa which were for years the dominant image of Africa seen on Western screens.

AFRICA THROUGH ALIEN LENSES

In order to delineate Sembene's role in the reshaping of Africa's portrayal on film, it is crucial first to establish the perceptions of sub-Saharan Africa that prevailed in motion pictures prior to his work. This provides an indispensable framework to the full understanding and appreciation of his films.

French feature films, especially, represented the trend with such productions as *L'Homme du Niger* (*The Man from Niger*, 1939), *Paysans Noirs* (*Black Peasants*, 1947), or *Nagana* (1955). British films of the colonial era also praised the merits of settlers and administrators whose task was to "civilise and uplift" the Africans. Other films, such as *Sanders of the River* (1935) and *King Solomon's Mines* (1937), used Africa merely as a background to the valiant deeds of European explorers winning over the African wilderness.

Unlike Europe, the United States had no direct colonial interest in Africa. For most Americans, Africa was a land of mystery penetrated only by daring white adventurers. Their impression of Africa had been molded primarily through images conveyed by the British through their history books or through romantic tales of adventures set in Africa by such authors as Sir Henry Rider Haggard, who wrote *King Solomon's Mines*, or Etherelda Lewis, a South African writer whose works were later to be adapted to the screen in the Hollywood production *Trader Horn* (1930). From reading such authors, the American writer Edgar Rice Burroughs, who never set foot in Africa, created the legendary character of Tarzan, whose heroic deeds have fascinated generations of young Americans. Burroughs's successful dime novels were to serve as a basis for some fifty Hollywood movies in which more care was devoted to the glorification of Tarzan than to a meaningful representation of Africa, except for the mythical quality of its wilderness in which the protagonist forever seems to be roaming free. As well as the Tarzan movies, a number of safari films and other jungle melodramas were produced on Hollywood assembly lines to appeal to the taste of cinema audiences for exoticism. The peak of those adventure melodramas was reached in the 1950s with films such as a new *King Solomon's Mines* (1950), a remake of the earlier British success, *The Snows of Kilimanjaro* (1952), *Mogambo* (1953), *Safari* (1955), *Roots of*

Heaven (1958), and others. These films made full use of technological advances in sound and color to depict African scenes and rhythms. They had in common amazingly unsurprising plots, and characters which were a reflection of America rather than Africa. Like his cowboy counterpart, the "great white hunter" of these adventure films was strong and highly skillful with firearms. He was many sided: pioneer, explorer, safari guide, and folk hero of a romantic story. He was the protagonist of a true morality tale ensuring the triumph of good over evil—the latter represented by ferocious animals and wicked natives. Africans themselves were either presented in demeaning servile roles or else functioned merely as a symbolic part of a hostile universe, which the great white hunter had to "tame" in a manner similar to the cowboy in the American West.

Documentary films, by definition, are generally meant to give a more accurate representation of reality than their fictional counterparts. It should be noted, however, that the early documentaries made about Africa suffered from the same condescending attitude towards this continent as did the feature films just mentioned. Their concern was mainly the picturesque "otherness" of Africa rather than a serious inquiry of its peoples and cultures. Thomas Cripps, an American historian who has researched extensively the various portrayals of blacks on U.S. screens, comments on those early ventures. "Their roots emerged from a faddish popular anthropology that had been a fountainhead of European exploration in Africa, complete with rival expeditions in search of the Nile, voyages to polar icecaps. . . . Therefore many early black figures on the screen were no more than the subjects of a quest for the legendary, the curious, and the bizarre, through darkest Africa and Carib Isle."[2]

If, indeed, American documentaries, such as *Theodore Roosevelt's Journey to Africa* or *The Military Drill of the Kikuyu Tribes and Other Native Ceremonies* (1914), provide us with interesting historical, sociological, and cultural elements concerning Africa, much less can be said of the French documentary *La Croisière Noire* (A Journey through Black Africa, 1924) made on the occasion of a Citroën rally in Africa. This film was designed to prove the triumph of French automobile technology under the most adverse circumstances. Other films, such as *Au Pays des Pygmées* (In the Pygmy Country, 1944) and *Les Grandes Chasses Africaines* (The Great African Safaris, 1944), intended as objective representations of African life, maintained a definite neutrality as to the exploitative methods of Western colonialism in the regions where those films were made. Except for *Voyage au Congo* (1927) by Marc Allégret, this non-commitment was so widespread that when René Vauthier started to make *Afrique 50* (1950), which dealt with the uprising of Africans against colonial rule in the Ivory Coast and the severe repression which ensued, he was ordered to discontinue filming, allegedly because he had not requested a filming permit. *Afrique 50* was then banned in France for many years because anything which might be a threat to the colonial order had to be suppressed. Another example of French control over documentaries on Africa is *Les Statues Meurent Aussi* (Statues Also Die, 1953), made by Alain Resnais and Chris Marker and allowed to be shown only ten years later in an abridged form. *Les Statues Meurent Aussi* illustrated the manner in which African art had been degraded by colonialism and was only shown after that system had ended in West Africa. A strong film, *Les Statues Meurent Aussi* remains, according to Ousmane Sembene and the French West Indian filmmaker Sarah Maldoror, the best film ever made on Africa, colonization, and traditional art objects. Yet other ethnographic films, such as Jean Rouch's earliest documentaries, could be "safely" released because they were Western inquiries into Africa's traditions rather than solely investigations of controversial contemporary issues.

In the area of documentary films about Africa, England possessed a more structured organization than France. The British government produced many "colonial" documentaries. Its Colonial Office created the Colonial Film Unit to show how progress could only be obtained through colonial rule. *Daybreak at Udi* (1949) is the best known among those documentaries because of its 1949 Academy Award for feature-length documentary picture. It was produced by the London's Crown

Film Unit in Nigeria to celebrate the victory of Western medicine over the staunch resistance of witch doctors. In the 1950s, *Salute to the Queen* recorded the loyalty of African subjects towards the British Crown, showing that all was well in the best of colonial worlds.

In the 1960s, Africa, along with many other areas of the world, was affected by the winds of political, economic, and technological change. It was thus to be expected that Western film would begin to reflect the new trends of world ideologies now associated with the political assertiveness of blacks within as well as outside the African continent. In the United States, for example, the emergence of a new black consciousness led a number of individuals and civil rights groups to criticize severely and to campaign actively in the media against the derogatory portrayals of Afro-Americans and Africans on Hollywood screens. In addition, the emerging independence of many African nations obviously clashed with the paternalistic views of Africa that previously dominated Western melodramas about Africa. As a result, the marketability of European and American jungle melodramas suffered, particularly in Africa itself. Furthermore, with the shift of interest to technological frontiers and the preoccupation of audiences with science, the older frontiers lost some of their fascination. Africa was no longer the primary source of mystery and mystique. Hollywood began to invest more in interplanetary conquests and more sophisticated horror films using the latest technological innovations to the comparative neglect of adventure movies set in Africa. Yet these factors seemingly affected the quantity of jungle melodramas produced more than their basic stereotyped qualities. These remained little changed as can be seen in such films as *Hatari* (1961), *Mr. Moses* (1965), *Africa Texas Style* (1967), *Tarzan and the Jungle Boy* (1967), or *Trader Horn* (1973), a remake of the American film released in 1930. Europe was equally slow in changing the mold in which its feature films about Africa were cast. In *Le Gentleman de Cocody* (1966), for example, the Ivory Coast provides an exotic and escapist background for Jean Marais's diamond-hunting tribulations, while in the 1964 British superproduction *Zulu*, a handful of valiant white soldiers are still stealing the show,

8   The Cinema of Ousmane Sembene

defeating thousands of barbarous natives. It was not until well into the 1970s that a new image of Africa began to appear in films such as *La Victoire en Chantant* (*Black and White in Color*, 1976), which parodied several aspects of French colonialism.

As Western feature films about Africa were decreasing in number, European and American filmmakers grew more interested in making documentaries about Africa in an attempt to investigate or record on film the political, economic, and cultural changes occurring in the newly emerging nations. They also became increasingly concerned with some of the richness of African culture that the West had previously disregarded. This new approach opened the way to more accurate and objective documentaries. Yet they were still made from a Western outlook, and some people like Ousmane Sembene regret that, under such "microscopic lenses," Africans were often studied "like insects." Jean Rouch, the French ethnologist turned filmmaker, recognizes his own limitations as an outsider striving to portray Africa. Of himself and other non-African filmmakers he wrote: "We will never be African and our films will remain films made by foreigners."[3]

Because of the limited distribution of documentaries usually aimed at a specialized audience (as in the case of ethnographic films), the representations of Africa which had the greatest impact on the largest number of people were the widely distributed African adventure melodramas manufactured in the 1950s and 1960s by the moguls of the Hollywood movie industry. In those motion pictures, the African setting propitious to the adventures of Western heroes was usually a static background denied the slighted social evolution and, thus, humanity. Africa, often seen in a global perspective, was fixed in time and "objectified" while its uni-dimensional natives seemed to be endlessly dancing and singing around a fire at midnight. It is to be observed that the shallowness of these African characters was analogous to that of Afro-American characters depicted by Hollywood at a time when Afro-Americans were mostly regarded as second-class citizens.[4] In those grandiose epics, Africans were primarily scenery props or unintelligent menials. Similar allegations were summarized by the Ethiopian filmmaker Haile Gerima.

Africa is generally a very good place for films. The Western filmmakers undermine our misery by putting us in the background, which is where we are in Western history. Africans are part of the landscape and they are used for a function—to bring an orange juice to the master—and they walk out of the scene. We are never human beings. We are underdeveloped characters, because they don't see us as part of a society.[5]

Africa's essence had been shunned on Western screens through films made by non-Africans, and in 1957 J. Koyinde Vaughan observed: "The future presentation on the screen of African life with the infinite possibilities of dramatizing both the past and the present as well as communicating to world audiences African inspirations can only be successfully achieved by Africans conscious of the great contribution that they must make to the art of cinema."[6]

Statements such as Vaughan's were not isolated and reflect a need most Africans feel deeply. This contention is bolstered by the fact that within only a few years, when new sociohistorical forces allowed them to do so, a number of Africans, among them Sembene, started to use film to explore the richness of their historical and cultural patrimony, as well as the complexities of their contemporary societies. It was expected that these filmmakers would bring into a new light the image of a continent which had been distorted through alien lenses for much too long.

AFRICA THROUGH AFRICAN LENSES

In outlining the images of Africa provided by African cinema, our attention will be focused on sub-Saharan Africa and essentially its Francophone areas. It is in this context that Sembene made his films. More than a geopolitical framework inherited from its colonial past, Francophone Africa is considered here as a cultural entity not only because French is the *lingua franca*, but because identical sociocultural patterns derive from a common past under French rule. The term "Francophone" will be used in a restrictive fashion with the exclusion of former Belgian colonies such as Zaire. The other reason for such a limitation lies in the fact that Francophone African cinema is eminently representative of African cinema. About 80 percent of indigenous sub-Saharan African films have been made in Francophone areas. As a whole, one observes a proportionally smaller number of films made in Anglophone Africa (independent countries formerly under British rule who have kept English as the official language), where directors have been encouraged to join television rather than to gamble in independent filmmaking.[7] There, film as a medium seems to reflect commercial patterns of Western cinema rather than a truly indigenous cultural essence, which is more appropriately diffused through popular Ghanaian or Nigerian theater productions or through established playwrights such as Wole Soyinka (Nigeria), J. P. Clark and Efua Sutherland (Ghana), and James Ngugi (Kenya).[8] The cinema of South Africa is also eliminated from our consideration since South Africa's desire to emulate Hollywood is essentially geared towards producing films faithful to the ideology of apartheid with little respect for black African life. Lusophone Africa, which only became independent in 1975, has produced an extremely limited number of films and will not likewise be a focal point in this thematic survey.

A Thematic Overview

At the beginning of film history, some North African filmmakers shared in the expansion of cinema. However, no such example can be found below the Sahara until the 1950s. This corroborates the statement by Koyinde Vaughan, according to whom "political development must . . . precede creative film production. It is difficult to imagine African filmmakers creating anything tangible under colonial tutelage."[9]

In spite of earlier beginnings like the twenty-minute black-and-white film *Afrique-sur-Seine* (Africa on the Seine, Senegal, 1955), made by a group of African students (including Paulin Soumanou Vieyra) about uprooted African youth in a foreign land, it was not until the early 1960s that African cinema emerged. This occurred at the same time as a number of new trends in film were becoming apparent in other countries such as the French "New Wave" or the Brazilian "Cinema Nôvo." Unlike the New Wave or Cinema Nôvo, however, African cinema developed out of no pre-existing tradition in filmmaking. It can be traced in part to the new-found independence which had come to most African countries around 1960. New nations were calling for new images and black Africans surrendered with enthusiasm to the appeal of film as a means of expression and communication because of its predictable impact on largely illiterate audiences. Thus, African cinema, and particularly Francophone African cinema, was to be given a pedagogical function as had been perceived by Vaughan in 1957 when he wrote: "In the field of education so necessary to Africa with its illiteracy problems, the cinema must occupy an important place. . . . This role must, however, be played by enlightened African cinema technicians."[10] This cinema was to become a cinema of awareness and protest. It was to highlight African culture and history and to denounce whatever could be a drawback to the harmonious evolution of African countries from colonial or neo-colonial bondage to full-fledged independent nations. In Ousmane Sembene's words, "we had to see, feel, and understand ourselves through the mirror of film. For us, African filmmakers, it was then necessary to become political, to become involved in a struggle against all the ills of man's cupidity, envy, individualism, the nouveau-riche mentality, and all the things we have inherited from the colonial and neo-colonial systems."[11]

Unlike Hollywood in style and purpose, Francophone African films are far from being glamorous, escapist, jungle melodramas. They are usually realistic and thoughtful low-budget films reflecting a variety of issues affecting contemporary Africa.

After the independence of their respective nations, African filmmakers were eager to celebrate on film their national sovereignty as a visual testimony for present and future generations. To commemorate the first anniversary of Senegal's independence, Paulin Soumanou Vieyra made *Une Nation est Née*

(A Nation Is Born, 20 minutes, 1961) about Senegalese history from French domination to self-determination. Yves Diagne shot *L'Afrique en Piste* (Africa Gets on the Track, 20 minutes, 1961), a film discussing the training of Senegalese athletes preparing for the Tokyo Olympic Games, thereby saluting the official entry of his country into the realm of international sports. Sekoumar Barry directed *Et Vint la Liberté* (And Then Freedom Came, 90 minutes, 1969), one of the many documentaries produced by Guinea to recount its transformations during the early years of its independence.

To recapture a past often distorted, blurred, or denied by the Western world was also a task these filmmakers assigned to themselves. It was in such a spirit that Ousmane Sembene devoted his first documentary, *L'Empire Sonhrai* (1963), and his latest feature film to date, *Ceddo* (1976), to the exploration of pre-colonial African history.[12] Likewise, with *La Rançon d'une Alliance* (The Price of a Union, 95 minutes, Congo, 1973), Sebastien Kamba describes the rivalry of two clans before the European colonization of Africa. Another film by Sembene, *Emitai* (95 minutes, 1971) is based on events which took place in Senegal during the Second World War.

Examining the past, African films also deal with a number of traditions still existing in today's world. Many films express the richness of African legends; for example, *Sur la Dune de la Solitude* (On the Dune of Solitude, 34 minutes, Ivory Coast, 1966) by Timité Bassori, *Deela* (30 minutes, Niger, 1969) by Mustapha Alassane, and *Ilombe* (90 minutes, Gabon, 1977), a feature film by Charles Mensah. African religious customs are illustrated in *Grand Magal à Touba* (The Great Pilgrimage to Touba, 25 minutes, Senegal, 1962) by Blaise Senghor, a documentary which depicts the annual pilgrimage of the Mourides (an Islamic sect) to the Great Mosque of Touba. *Sous le Signe du Vodoun* (Under the Sign of Voodoo, 100 minutes, Benin, 1973) by Pascal Abikanlou shows the influence of traditional African religions in a contemporary milieu. The socioreligious ritual of circumcision is reviewed in *Tiyabu Biru* (Circumcision, 90 minutes, 1977), the first feature film by Moussa Bathily of Mali. Traditional African sculpture is celebrated by Yves Diagne in *Delou Thyossane* (Back to the Sources,

12 minutes, Senegal, 1966) while ancestral African dances are recorded for posterity in *Sindiely* (11 minutes, Senegal, 1963) by Paulin Soumanou Vieyra, *Tam Tam à Paris* (African Drums in Paris, 30 minutes, Cameroon, 1963) by Thérèse Sita Bella, and *Les Ballets de la Forêt Sacrée* (Dances from the Sacred Forest, 25 minutes, Senegal, 1970) by Abdou Fary Faye. Similarly, the cultural significance of traditional Casamance wrestling and customary Wolof games is demonstrated by Momar Thiam in *Luttes Casamançaises* (Casamance Wrestling, 18 minutes, Senegal, 1968) and *Simb ou les Jeux du Faux Lion* (Simb or the False Lion's Games, 12 minutes, Senegal, 1969), respectively.

Yet in spite of an undeniable reverence for their cultural patrimony, Francophone African filmmakers focus, with genuine concern and often a critical eye, on the anachronistic nature of some African traditions in a contemporary environment. Some films, like *Kodou* (100 minutes, Senegal, 1971) by Ababacar Samb offer an ambivalent standpoint concerning this issue but, at the same time, other motion pictures point out that changes must definitely be envisioned to ensure the insertion of Africa into a modern context. The customs of arranged marriage, polygamy, excessive dowry, and the ostracism against illegitimate children is respectively denounced in *Muna Moto* (The Other's Child, 100 minutes, Cameroon, 1975) by Jean Pierre Dikongue-Pipa, *Le Wazou du Polygame* (The Polygamist's Morale, 50 minutes, Niger, 1970) by Oumarou Ganda, *Sey Seyeti* (Husband and Wives, 90 minutes, Senegal, 1980) by Ben Diogaye Beye, *Pousse-Pousse* (Pedicab, 90 minutes, Cameroon, 1976) by Daniel Kamwa, and *Nous Sommes Tous Coupables* (We Are All Guilty, 105 minutes, Mali, 1980), a feature film by Falaba Issa Traoré. In a like manner, *O'Bali* (120 minutes, Gabon, 1976) by Pierre Marie Dong addresses ancestral mores according to which a deceased wife must be replaced by a woman from her own family. In *Abusuan* (The Family, 90 minutes, Ivory Coast, 1972) and *L'Herbe Sauvage* (Wild Grass, 95 minutes, Ivory Coast, 1978), Henri Duparc condemns the abuse of family solidarity whenever it leads to the shameless exploitation by family members of individuals who show some financial success. Then, feature films like *Le*

Sang des Parias (The Pariahs' Blood, 80 minutes, Upper Volta, 1972) by Mamadou Kola Djim, *Wamba* (Between Water and Fire, 91 minutes, Mali, 1976) by Alkaly Kaba, *Djelli* (90 minutes, Ivory Coast, 1980) by Kramo Lancine Fadika, and *Adja Tio* (100 minutes, Ivory Coast, 1980) by Jean Louis Koula blame the social inequities resulting from the caste system. Finally, a critical view of religion is to be found in several African productions: *Saitane* (Satan, 55 minutes, Niger, 1973) by Oumarou Ganda indicts the abuses exerted through animism, while *Njangaan* (The Koranic School Student, 90 minutes, Senegal, 1975) attacks the misuse of Islam.

Contrary to Western directors, who have mainly depicted Africa as an immutable continent, Francophone African filmmakers are primarily interested in reflecting its transition from tradition to modernity. They tend to focus on the contemporary sociopolitical and economical forces at work on particular groups of people in designated geographic areas. As such, they investigate specific topics related to these forces.

Since the great majority of Africans live in rural areas, the attention given by these filmmakers to rural life is not surprising. Pascal Abikanlou describes his native village in *Ganvié, Mon Village* (Ganvié, My Village, 24 minutes, Benin, 1968) and Thierno Sow illustrates the life of a Senegalese peasant in *La Journée de Djibril N'Diaye, Paysan Sénégalais* (The Day of Djibril N'Diaye, A Senegalese Farmer, 60 minutes, Senegal, 1969). Mustapha Alassane uses the subterfuge of an African legend in *Toula ou le Génie des Eaux* (Toula or the Water Spirit, 90 minutes, Niger, 1973) to state that the problem of drought could be resolved if adequate means were used by local governments or international organizations. Safi Faye, the Senegalese woman filmmaker, stresses the precariousness of rural life in *Kaddu Beykat* (*News from the Village*, 100 minutes, 1974) and *Fadjal* (Recent Arrival, 30 minutes, 1979), while her compatriot Ousmane William M'Baye presents a fictional examination of the exploitation of farmers by co-operatives in *Doomi Ngatch* (The Child from Njatch, 30 minutes, 1979). The implantation of new agricultural methods often has severe sociocultural repercussions. This is shown by Djibril Kouyaté in *Le*

Retour de Tiéman (Tiéman's Return, 30 minutes, Mali, 1962) and by Cheikh Ngaido Bah in his docu-drama *Rewo Dande Mayo* (On the Other Side of the River, 60 minutes, 1979), a film commissioned by Mauritania. The introduction of industrial fishing techniques and their effects on local fishermen is reviewed in *Gety Tey* (30 minutes, Senegal, 1979) by Samba Felix Ndiaye. Wishing to escape the uncertainty of life in rural areas, many villagers migrate to large cities. Thus, the problems caused by the displacement of people from village to town are illustrated by Mahama Johnson Traoré in his feature length film *Garga M'Bossé* (Cactus, 80 minutes, Senegal, 1974) and by Safi Faye in her documentary *Selbé* (30 minutes, Senegal, 1982).

Like many African writers, African directors touch upon the fate of people ill prepared for urban life. In *Borom Sarret* (20 minutes, 1963) Ousmane Sembene relates the frustrating day of a Dakar cartman whose trade is obsolete. In *La Brosse* (The Brush, 15 minutes, Senegal, 1974), Cheikh Ngaido Bah describes the hardships suffered by a young shoeshine boy who helps support his family. A similar theme is featured in *Samba Talli* (The Bum, 20 minutes, Senegal, 1975) by Ben Diogaye Beye. *Taw* (24 minutes, 1970), by Sembene, depicts a young man faced with unemployment in Dakar. Frequently, African cities are seen as places of perdition for recent migrants who occasionally resort to theft or prostitution for survival. Souleymane Cissé illustrates juvenile delinquency in *Cinq Jours d'une Vie* (Five Days in a Life, 50 minutes, Mali, 1972), while Momar Thiam tackles the same issue in *Baks* (Hashish, 90 minutes, Senegal, 1974). *Le Cri du Muezzin* (The Muezzin's Call, 45 minutes, Ivory Coast, 1972) by N'Dabian Vodio, offers a critical analysis of the Ivorian society in stressing the marginal life of prostitutes, thieves, and murderers. The topic of female prostitution is found in *Le Destin* (Fate, 90 minutes, Niger, 1976) by Diambéré Sega Coulibaly and *Le Prix de la Liberté* (The Price of Freedom, 90 minutes, Cameroon, 1977) by Jean Pierre Dikongue Pipa. Returning to the village after trying experiences in the city is occasionally advocated by a few directors who recall, sometimes with oversentimentality, rural areas as a more natural and favorable atmosphere for human growth. Such a position was taken by Gnoan M'Bala in *Amanie* (What News, 32 minutes, Ivory Coast, 1972). The West had mainly perceived African women as sensuous creatures with exposed breasts or as submissive daughters and wives in portrayals which denied the important role they play in African families. Now, women's issues are examined with great care as in *Diègue-Bi* (The Young Woman, 80 minutes, Senegal, 1970), a sequel to *Diankha-Bi* (The Young Girl, 55 minutes, Senegal, 1969). Both of these films by Mahama Johnson Traoré center on the changing status of the Senegalese woman at the various stages of her life in the midst of a patriarchal society undergoing significant mutations. Souleymane Cissé's *Den Muso* (The Girl, 90 minutes, Mali, 1975) depicts the misfortunes of a young unwed pregnant woman in a Malian context. Several portrayals of African women are represented in *Xala* (116 minutes, 1974) by Ousmane Sembene, *L'Etoile Noire* (The Black Star, 100 minutes, Niger, 1975) by Djinga-Reye Maiga, *Le Chapeau* (The Hat, 70 minutes, Ivory Coast, 1975) by Gnoan M'Bala, and *Ayouma* (80 minutes, Gabon, 1977), a feature film by Pierre Marie Dong. The reinstatement of a Westernized African woman in a traditional society is scrutinized in *Notre Fille* (Our Daughter, 100 minutes, Cameroon, 1980), a fictional film by Daniel Kamwa.

The acute question of illiteracy which still affects about 80 percent of the African people is given attention to in Yaya Kossoko's *La Réussite de Meithèbre* (Meithèbre's Success, 20 minutes, Niger, 1970) and Ousmane Sembene's *Mandabi* (The Money Order, 105 minutes, 1968). The need for adult education is reflected through *Le Certificat* (The Diploma, 95 minutes, Senegal, 1980), a feature film by Tidiane Aw.

The new, indigenous bourgeoisie which has emerged in African nations since the 1960s is also the frequent target of filmmakers who accuse them of nepotism, corruption, and mismanagement of the economy of their country. Films expressing such opinions include: *F.V.V.A.* (Femme, Voiture, Villa, Argent—Wife, Car, Villa, Money, 75 minutes, Niger, 1970) by Mustapha Alassane, *Sérigne Assane* (For Those Who Know, 80 minutes, Senegal, 1971) by Tidiane Aw, *Lambaaye* (Graft, 80 minutes, Senegal, 1972) by Mahama Johnson Traoré, *Xala* by Ousmane Sembene, *Le Nouveau Venu* (The Newcomer, 87 minutes, Benin, 1976) by Richard de Meideros, and *Baara* (Work, 90 minutes, Mali, 1977) and *Finyé* (The Wind, 100 minutes, Mali, 1982) both by Souleymane Cissé. *En Résidence Surveillée* (Under House Arrest, 90 minutes, Senegal, 1981), the first feature film by Paulin Soumanou Vieyra, focuses on a *coup d'état*, political plotting, and the role of foreign advisors in an imaginary country. Yet the theme of this film is a composite of events which actually occurred in various African nations. Never before had an African filmmaker dealt with such a sensitive topic.

One can say that the overall subject which characterizes African films is the conflictive dichotomy existing between traditional Africa and the Western ways by which it is increasingly permeated. This cleavage is related through *Contras City* (27 minutes, Senegal, 1968) by Djibril Diop Mambety. *Mouna ou le Rêve d'un Artiste* (Mouna, an Artist's Dream, 55 minutes, Ivory Coast, 1969) by Henri Duparc and *Les Tams Tams se sont Tus* (Drums Stopped Playing, 90 minutes, Gabon, 1972) by Philippe Mory stress the alienation of traditional sculptors in the face of Western commercialism. *Touki Bouki* (The Hyena's Journey, 90 minutes, Senegal, 1973), also by Djibril Diop Mambety, is an allegory based on the dream of a former shepherd and the matter of his survival in an alien urban environment.

Besides the sociopsychological alienation some Africans may endure in their own society, their alienation in foreign countries is pointed out in Jean Paul N'Gassa's *Aventure en France* (Adventure in France, 28 minutes, Cameroon, 1962), Urbain Dia Mokouri's *Point de Vue* (Point of View, 16 minutes, Cameroon, 1965), Ousmane Sembene's *La Noire de* (Black Girl, 60 minutes, 1966). Désiré Ecaré's *Concerto pour un Exil* (Concerto for an Exile, 42 minutes, Ivory Coast, 1967), Amadou S. Camara's *Ame Perdue* (Lost Soul, 28 minutes, Guinea, 1969), Safi Faye's *La Passante* (The Passerby, 10 minutes, Senegal, 1972), and Ben Diogaye Beye's *Les Princes Noirs de St. Germain des Prés* (The Black Princes of St. Germain des Prés, 20 minutes, Senegal, 1976). *Soleil O* (O Sun, 100 minutes, 1971) and *Les Bicots Nègres Vos Voisins* (Dirty Arabs, Dirty Niggers, Your Neighbors, 110 minutes, 1973), produced in France by the Mauritanian filmmaker Med Hondo, reflect the plight of African laborers in Paris while addressing the sociopolitical and economic patterns of their migration. Through *Nationalité: Immigré* (Citizenship: Immigrant, 90 minutes, 1974) and *Safrana ou le Droit à la Parole* (Safrana; Or, the Right to Speak, 110 minutes, 1974), Sidney Sokhona, also of Mauritania, describes African workers in France and their growing political awareness. *L'Homme d'Ailleurs* (The Foreigner, Ivory Coast, 1980) is a fiction film by Mory Traoré which relates the fatal outcome of the estrangement of an African exiled in Japan. *Moi, ta Mère* (I, Your Mother, 60 minutes, Senegal, 1981), a documentary, by Safi Faye, deals with the condition of African workers in Germany.

Another category of films are those which treat the readjustment problems of the newly returned Africans to their environment, like *Et la Neige n'était plus* (There Was No Longer Snow, 24 minutes, Senegal, 1965) by Ababacar Samb, *Le Retour de l'Aventurier* (The Adventurer's Return, 55 minutes, Niger, 1966) by Mustapha Alassane, *Mon Stage en France* (My Training in France, 25 minutes, Cameroon, 1968) by Thomas Makoulet Manga, and *Cabascabo* (52 minutes, Niger, 1969) by Oumarou Ganda.

Finally, the films of Sarah Maldoror, a Guadeloupean director of African descent, also should be included in this core of Francophone films because most of her works are largely relevant to Africans in Africa, as is the case of *Sambizanga* (1972), a feature film which denounces the abuses of colonialism.

This thematic overview indicates that the same topics are consistently treated in African films, particularly Sembene's ones, over more than two decades. They include rural underdevelopment, the introduction of new agricultural and fishing methods, rural migration, the poverty of urban masses, unemployment, juvenile delinquency, prostitution, cultural and social alienation, the status of women, illiteracy and education, the corruption of the new elite in power, political instability, and emigration. And, if film is to be considered a cultural reflector for sociopolitical analysis, one may assume that most of the issues stressed in the 1960s were still far from being resolved in Francophone Africa twenty years later.

Difficulties Faced by Sembene and Other African Filmmakers

Besides their realistic portrayal of Africa, African films also differ from Western productions because they are made within a context which is radically different from that of Western filmmaking.

A first handicap which Francophone African filmmakers have had to face is the lack of an infrastructure needed for the full development of a film industry. This paucity of equipment was inherited from the colonial era. One can assume that since films made by Africans were a potential threat to her colonial system, France showed little interest in training African directors and in setting up film structures in her African territories. As a result, the task of early African filmmakers after the independence of their countries was considerably complicated.

In creating films which would reveal the authenticity of Africa, Francophone filmmakers were investigating a virgin realm. The existing cinema, as a means of expression and communication, was an art that existed outside their culture and concerns, an imported art in which Africans had participated as objects and not as subjects. They had to decolonize the cinema and adapt it to the reality and needs of Africa. More often than not, this reality meant the mere availability of a single 16 mm camera, leftover black-and-white film footage from Western movie crews working in Africa, and their own meager resources.

In the 1960s, many African countries were still culturally and economically dependent on former colonial powers. Since no film school existed in sub-Saharan Francophone Africa, the majority of African directors acquired their skills abroad within a variety of ideological frameworks. Some of them, like Ousmane Sembene and Souleymane Cissé, who received a scholarship to the Moscow Film School, studied in the U.S.S.R.; but as expected, a number of directors went to France for their education in film. Then, as the years went by, these filmmakers trained new technicians and directors on the set.

In the beginning, with only a few exceptions (for example, Guinea), local filmmaking received little official encouragement, since governments did not consider film an essential priority in their development planning. Consequently, some filmmakers, like Sembene, were initially supported, financially and technically, by the French Ministry of Cooperation. This explains why their early works are in French: money was allocated after acceptance of the script or else the copyright of the film was bought after it was made. It should be noted here that France's interest in sponsoring African films has been sustained throughout the years since, and even now various African works are being co-produced with this French government agency.

Later, a few African directors such as Ousmane Sembene, Souleymane Cissé, Ababacar Samb, Mahama Johnson Traoré, and others, aspiring to exert more control over the production and distribution of their films, created their own film companies. However, the films produced by these independent filmmakers also required additional private and/or government funding.

A second constraint on African filmmakers has been that of finance. The budgets of Francophone African films were and remain tiny compared with those in Western filmmaking. This scarcity of financial resources has been a serious drawback for most directors who have often had to personally back the funding of their productions. Sembene, for instance, had to mortgage his house to make *Ceddo*. As a result, no independent filmmaker has been solely sustained by film profits because they are generally reinvested in subsequent works. Sembene has to rely on his book royalties, lecture fees, and other personal means; Vieyra is employed by the Senegalese Ministry of Information; Mahama Johnson Traoré operates a photo shop in Dakar; and Med Hondo dubs films in France.

Likewise, Francophone African filmmakers are hampered by an insufficiency of local technicians and the scarcity of film labs in Africa. Thus, foreign technicians often have to be flown to

Africa, and film processing is usually done in European countries—all of which increases film cost. Since processing is done abroad, the immediate screening of rushes as is done in Western cinema to permit the correction of possible flaws through subsequent retakes is impossible. This affects the quality of the final product. Sembene's *Emitai* includes overexposed scenes which might have been avoided had the film been processed locally. Maintenance of film equipment in Africa also poses a certain number of problems because of adverse climatic conditions such as excessive heat, humidity, or sand dust.

A further obstacle to the development of the indigenous cinema industry is the monopolistic structure of the distribution network. Apart from commercial successes like *Xala*, independently produced and distributed films generally reach a limited number of African viewers. Yet film audiences are large in Africa, especially in urban areas whose populations have increased with migration and where cinema and soccer have now become people's main collective source of entertainment. Contrary to what has happened in many Western countries, television watching in Africa is still far from competing with movie going, due both to the high price of TV sets and the low quality of programming. However, this urban market is not readily opened to films made by Africans because of the stronghold of expatriate distribution companies with a financial interest in promoting foreign films. In the early 1970s, Pierre Pommier noted that among the films shown in Francophone sub-Sahara Africa, 50 to 55 percent were American and mostly westerns, 30 to 35 percent were French and largely detective films or war movies, and 15 percent were Indian, Egyptian, or Italian.[13]

Indeed, local filmmakers who, for the most part, are small independent entrepreneurs have found it hard to challenge the power of foreign monopolies such as the Compagnie Africaine Cinématographique Industrielle (COMACICO), the Société d'Exploitation Cinématographique Africaine (SECMA), and Afro-American Films (AFRAM, established in 1969 by the powerful Motion Picture Export Association of America, the MPEAA, to distribute films in Francophone Africa).

SECMA and its affiliates have specialized in the distribution of American movies, while COMACICO and its associates seem to focus on the importation of French, Indian, and Arab films. In 1974, each of these companies owned about one-fifth of the 240 movie theaters operating in Francophone West Africa, while the others, usually smaller, were for the most part owned and managed by other foreign companies like the Union Générale Cinématographique (UGC), or controlled by Lebanese, Syrian, and African interests.

In the same manner as European trading companies used to operate in the colonial period, SECMA and COMACICO have their headquarters in Europe (Monaco) where they direct their profits, rarely investing them in Africa except for the taxes required by African governments on imported products. Even though *Diegue-Bi* by Mahama Johnson Traoré was co-produced with SECMA and *Mandabi* by Sembene was distributed by COMACICO, these companies are generally not interested in promoting Francophone African cinema because of the limited number of local films and the irregularity of their production. The practice of double feature screenings which prevails throughout Francophone Africa also excludes the possibility of the presentation of the many short films made by African filmmakers. Finally, the strong sociopolitical content of most African films is usually considered a handicap to their profitability, while escapist foreign films ensure safe financial returns. Francophone Africa is thus more a consumer than a producer of films: approximately 500 new films are shown each year, while only about 300 African films have been shot in twenty years. In 1972, Vieyra estimated that a cumulative total of 3,000 films (new and second run) had been distributed that year on the African continent of which only 60 had been produced in Africa.[14]

More interested in profit than culture, SECMA and COMACICO, through their various distribution strategies, have oriented the African public's tastes towards action films (westerns, European historical romances, detective films, and, more recently, Kung-fu movies), melodramas (Indian and Egyptian sagas), or inept comedies (mostly European), imposing on audiences Western patterns inherently alien to Africa. These films are dubbed in French rather than subtitled be-

Background 23

cause of the generally high rate of illiteracy in Francophone Africa. French being understood and spoken by less than a third of the population in those regions, most viewers have a predilection for films emphasizing actions rather than character analysis. The popularity of Indian and Arab melodramas is usually attributed to visual and cultural patterns comparable to those of Africa (festivals, dances, rituals, and so on). Foreign films divert the public's mind from the problems existing in their society and African audiences have been more eager to see entertainment films than those which require a certain amount of reflection.

In addition to the lack of interest shown by foreign distribution companies, the early African filmmakers had to face the indifference of many African governments concerning the promotion of independent local cinema. In several instances, the films produced by ministries of information were no more than propagandist pictures showing the travels and addresses of political leaders. It was only later that supporting agencies like the Société Ivoirienne du Cinéma (SIC), the Société Nationale du Cinéma (SNC) of Senegal (replaced in 1977 by a national film fund), the Office Cinématographique du Mali (OCINAM), the Office Béninois du Cinéma (OBECI), and the Société Nationale du Cinéma Voltaïque (SONAVOCI) were created to control film imports and to facilitate the production, distribution, and export of indigenous films. This happened in Benin, where COMACICO was replaced by OBECI, and in Senegal, where the Société d'Importation de Distribution et d'Exploitation Cinématographique (SIDEC) was created in 1974. The SIDEC, in which the Senegalese government holds 80 percent of the shares, has had a significant impact in Senegal, where 8 percent of the films shown must be African.

Because of the small size of most Francophone African nations, with populations ranging from 1 to 6 million, the future of local films is more and more seen in terms of regional agreements. In 1974, African leaders belonging to the Organisation Commune Africaine et Mauricienne (OCAM) decided to create the Consortium Inter Africain de Distribution Cinématographique (CIDC) and the Centre Inter Africain de Production de Films (CIPROFILMS) with headquarters in Upper

Volta. Such initiatives were supported by international organizations like UNESCO in the hope of developing in Ouagadougou the sorely needed processing, editing, and studio facilities that would enable African filmmakers from fifteen countries to complete their films in Africa while expanding their distribution channels both in Africa and abroad.

As they gradually became aware of the importance of film as a medium, most new African governments realized its latent power as a channel of political dissent. Thus, they sought means of control which often degenerated into censorship. They established mechanisms for controlling the content of the films that were produced or distributed. Since sex and violence are not usually found in African films, their restraints were mainly directed at any political overtones that challenged the dominant ideology. Thus, Sembene's *Ceddo*, about Catholic and Muslim imperialism in seventeenth-century Senegal, was banned for eight years in Senegal. The reason given for its rejection was that its title did not follow government standards concerning the spelling of "Ceddo," which officials insisted should only take one "d." It hardly seems likely, however, that linguistic preoccupations about such a minor matter would lead to the suppression of a film, and it seems more probable that *Ceddo* was censored for religious or political reasons. Mahama Johnson Traoré also suffered censorship with *Lambaaye* and *Réou Takh* (*Big City*, 45 minutes, Senegal, 1972). Both films, which are severely critical of Senegal's political and economic situation, have not yet been allowed for public viewing in that country.

Senegal's example has been followed by many other Francophone African countries where films are subject to a double censorship: first when screenplays are reviewed for the allocation of complementary funds and shooting permits and then when films receive ratings and screening authorizations with or without suggested modifications (editing of scenes, sequences, and so on). Because of this official censorship, some filmmakers apply a form of self-censorship when the content of their work appears to be too controversial. Thus, they set their plots in the past, reflecting contemporary issues through the mirror of history. Otherwise, they illustrate tales with subtle metaphorical analogies to render issues more palatable to official authorities.

These directors also have to face a difficult choice concerning language. They can use French, which limits the African audiences but permits a wider circulation abroad, or they can use a local language that gains a greater indigenous audience at the cost of overseas markets and at the risk of favoring one ethnic group over others. Sembene feels that Senegalese reality is better expressed in an African language rather than an alien tongue inherited from colonialism. His is a cultural and political stand against the linguistic influence of France in independent Senegal. Although he made his very early films in French, Sembene shot *Mandabi* in two versions, one in French and one in Wolof, a language understood by 90 percent of the Senegalese people. Then, except for *Xala*, in which French is largely used to reflect the alienation of the principal character, his subsequent films have been in Diola (*Emitai*) or Wolof (*Taw, Ceddo*) with French or English subtitles. Safi Faye also favors the use of Wolof in her films. Many other African filmmakers have adopted African languages in their works: Oumarou Ganda shot *Cabascabo* in Hausa; Souleymane Cissé used Bambara in *Den Muso, Baara*, and *Finyé*; and Moussa Bathily made *Tiyabu Biru* in Sarakholé. Yet even in 1980, many directors, such as Henri Duparc and Pierre Marie Dong, still favored French. They argue that an African language is limited to one geographical area and that subtitles in French can be read only by a minority.

These various problems pertaining to production, distribution, audience, censorship, and language constitute the socioeconomic, political, and cultural constraints within which Sembene and other filmmakers have to work. It is only by understanding these difficulties that one can adequately appreciate the cinema of Ousmane Sembene and his role as a griot filmmaker in the development of African film.

NOTES

1. From a series of interviews with Ousmane Sembene conducted by the author in Senegal in 1978.

2. Thomas Cripps, *Black Film as Genre* (Bloomington: Indiana University Press, 1979), pp. 13–14.

3. Jean Rouch, "L'Afrique entre en Scène," *Le Courrier de l'Unesco*, n. 3 (1962), p. 15.

4. For more information pertaining to such a comparison see Daniel J. Leab, *From Sambo to Superspade* (Boston: Houghton Mifflin Co., 1976).

5. Françoise Pfaff, "Toward a New Era in Cinema," *New Directions*, vol. 4, n. 3 (1977), p. 28.

6. J. Koyinde Vaughan, "Africa South of the Sahara and the Cinema," *Présence Africaine*, n. 14–15 (1957), pp. 220–21.

7. Television and laboratories for the processing of black-and-white films had been established by the British in Africa before it occurred in Francophone Africa. The first television station was created in western Nigeria as early as October 1959. Other channels were to follow in that country with the help of British and American corporations which foresaw outlets for their products. Later, Nigeria "Nigerianized" its television and exerted more control over its television programs, which were subsequently to include screen adaptations of works by Nigerian writers and playwrights more relevant to the Nigerian reality.

In an interview with the author in February 1978, Paulin Soumanou Vieyra stated:

Anglophone Africans got television before the Francophone Africans. According to my own experience in this field, television trains civil servants for a career in which creativity is not always of primary importance. In Ghana or Nigeria, almost all directors are involved in television and neglect cinema, an area in which Francophone African directors are stronger due perhaps to a later development of television in their countries.

One of the best known Anglophone African filmmakers is Ola Balogun of Nigeria. Other directors are Segun Olusola and Alhaji Adamu Halilu (Nigeria), Kwate Nee Owoo, Aryetey Sam, Kwah Ansah, and James King Ampaw (Ghana).

8. The popular rural and urban drama of Anglophone Africa includes plays staged by the Yorouba Opera, the Ogunde Theatre Troupe, and the Ghanaian Concert Parties.

9. J. Koyinde Vaughan, "Africa South of the Sahara and the Cinema," p. 221.

10. Ibid.

11. Sembene to author, Senegal, 1978.

12. The Sonhrai are an Islamic African ethnic group who occupy

the middle reaches of the Niger river. The Sonhrai empire was at its peak during the sixteenth and seventeenth centuries and then crumbled due to a succession of invasions and internal dissensions. The prosperity of the Sonhrai empire derived from its geographical location, which allowed it to control the trade routes going from Mali to the Maghrib and Egypt.

13. Pierre Pommier, *Cinéma et Développement en Afrique Noire Francophone* (Paris: Pédone, 1974), p. 16.

14. Paulin Soumanou Vieyra, "Le Deuxième Festival Cinématographique de Tachkent," *Présence Africaine*, n. 83 (1972), p. 87.

2
SEMBENE, A GRIOT OF MODERN TIMES

On many occasions, Sembene has drawn a parallel between the traditional storyteller and the modern African filmmaker in terms such as these: "The artist must in many ways be the mouth and the ears of his people. In the modern sense, this corresponds to the role of the griot in traditional African culture. The artist is like a mirror. His work reflects and synthesizes the problems, the struggles, and the hopes of his people."[1]

To fully grasp the importance of these words, one must refer to the essence of Africa's oral tradition of which the griot is an eminent representative. According to Georges Balandier and Jacques Maquet, the word *griot* comes from the Portuguese word *criado*, which means servant, or from the French corruption of the Wolof word *gewel*, which refers to the members of a caste formerly attached to a family or a clan.[2] "They are to be found either at the courts of chiefs or established on their own in towns and villages, acting as story-tellers, clowns, heralds, genealogists, musicians, oral reporters, or paid flatterers or insulters."[3]

Elolongué Epanya Yondo of Cameroon writes that the griots are professionals who specialize in storytelling, reciting legends, or recounting the valiant deeds of a family's or country's forebears. Griots may be the chroniclers of an important family or of a group of people—like the Bambara hunters' griot—or itinerant poets and musicians who extol the praises of the person who has hired them for a special festivity.[4] Dorothy S. Blair, who translated into English *Birago Diop's Tales of Amadou Koumba* stresses in her foreword that, "in the French-speaking territories of West Africa today, especially in Guinea and Senegal, the griot is an important and respected member of the artistic and cultural community."[5]

Yet the griot has an ambiguous status. While he enjoys freedom of expression and respect for his knowledge from both the elite and the masses, he is also stigmatized because he belongs to an inferior caste within Senegalese society. Although Mbye B. Cham agrees with the general definitions of griots he also makes a very important distinction between two kinds of griot found in Wolof society: the gewel and the *lebkat*. The gewel is someone who possesses "mastery over the word and knowledge" by social tradition and training (craft transmitted within a cast from generation to generation), while the lebkat is a raconteur whose storytelling can be performed at any time by any member of a given community—heads of families or women, especially in such countries as Senegal.[6] Also, it often happens that the professional griot looks down upon the lebkat's storytelling. Yet both the gewel and the lebkat are the repositories of Africa's oral treasures, the collective product of a common experience.

The oral tradition embodied by the griot or the conveying of information and memories orally has existed in all societies at one stage or another of history when spoken words and gestures were more important than graphic signs. In all areas of the world, mankind has first expressed itself through the spoken word before inventing a writing system. One remembers that the epics of ancient Greece, such as the *Iliad* and *Odyssey*, were transmitted orally before being codified in writing. Although the oral tradition is by no means limited to Africa, it is there that it probably remains the most popular and the most vital today.

Until recently, the verbal richness of black Africa was found outside of books. It was kept alive in people's minds and expressed in specific circumstances such as festivals or evening storytelling sessions by professional or extemporaneous performers. In Africa, oral literature is still very much a part of a deep-rooted collective custom, adapted to a communal, largely illiterate, and agriculturally based society. Through its myths, legends, epics, tales, or historical poems, it has celebrated the prowess of kings and warriors, perpetuated its past, and preserved its ancestral wisdom while strengthening the sociocultural and historical identity of the group. The story is probably the most common and the most appreciated literary genre of black Africa's oral tradition.

If "in the beginning there was the word," African storytellers have since made ample use of it, and their influence has gone beyond Africa into Europe and the Americas. The findings of the English linguist Alice Werner prove that their stories were the source of Aesop's fables—whose name derives from "Ethiop," a general term for "black African" in Greek antiquity—which in turn influenced La Fontaine's fables. The folk literature of the New World is also immensely enriched by its African heritage via the slave trade.

It is true that the love of telling and listening to stories is a universal human characteristic, yet equally undeniable is the fact that it is becoming less and less prevalent in industrialized societies. In such societies, television has become a surrogate storyteller presenting children with cartoons and other stories which are but modernized tales. At one time or another, tales full of magic and spirits have been spread all over the world. Yet it is in countries such as Africa that it is still widely appreciated.

"Africa is the land of story-tellers and tales," asserts Georges Balandier,[7] while Elolongué Epanya Yondo underlines that "the tale is the nurturing breast which feeds most of the Negro African literary genres."[8] The presence in African cinema of tales and oral stories adapted to the screen comes as no surprise in films by Momar Thiam or Mustapha Alassane. One also notes that the atmosphere of film screening parallels the traditional time for much of storytelling at gatherings when the family or community meets. Now it is left to determine how and to what extent African film, as a means of expression and communication, is indebted to the oral tradition. According to Alphonse

Raphaël N'Diaye from Senegal, "... the oral traditions constitute the global expression of the life of our people."[9] Besides, in a Western frame of reference, Joseph M. Boggs also emphasizes the storytelling aspect of film: "Although film is a unique medium, with properties and characteristics which set it apart from other art forms such as painting, sculpture, fiction and drama, it is also, in its most popular and powerful form, a story-telling medium."[10] Thus, because of structural similarities to the medium of the tale, film is the ideal means of conveying the treasures and techniques of the African oral tradition. If indeed most films tell stories, their content and form are determined by a broader cultural context; that is, the traditions and needs of a given society. This is precisely what the Ethiopian filmmaker Haile Gerima implies in his observation: "The oral tradition is a part of African film aesthetics in terms of space, pace, and rhythms."[11]

Most contemporary African artists draw on their heritage while associating their traditions with Western models. For instance, both African writers and filmmakers illustrate African themes through forms and/or tools which are not indigenous to their culture—be it the novel or the camera. They introduce the same symbiosis in art as that which is unavoidable in their transitional African society based on both African and Western patterns. It is natural, therefore, that Sembene, in addition to defining himself as a griot, should provide works whose style and themes derive from Africa's oral tradition.

The griot is physically present in a number of Sembene's films. He is shown performing varied functions as the actor/narrator of *Niaye* and the cart driver's family griot in *Borom Sarret*. In *Xala*, griots are also part of a celebration following the "Senegalization" of the Chamber of Commerce and of El Hadji's wedding festivities. In *Ceddo*, Fara, a griot, follows the princess and her captor.

Sembene's films, like the griot's renditions, provide the immediacy of visual and auditory action. Thus, when he presents and discusses his works with various groups of viewers in Senegal, Sembene arouses a dynamic interchange with the audience, somewhat re-establishing the verbal directness which has always existed between the griot and the spectators.

Indeed, Sembene's works, like those of other African directors, are accessible to popular audiences because they represent a collective experience based on visual and aural elements with characteristics which can be compared to the griot's delivery. Anyone who has attended a film screening in a working-class district of Senegal is struck by the intensely vocal participation of the viewers who comment on the plot of the film, respond to one another's remark, address the actors, and laugh at their mishaps just as they would during the griot's performance in which dramatic mimics and gestures are used to encourage audience reaction.

"Sembene Ousmane is a born story-teller," observed a film critic in the early stages of the Senegalese director's career.[12] No one could refute such an assertion. As a modern griot, Sembene performs the ritual incantation of images and words which link reality to metaphor in the creative process which constitutes a work of art. In terms of style and content, the griot's handling of social satire in African societies is legendary. The songs and tales of traditional folklore make ample use of comic gestures, words, and situations. The griot is known to have the unique capability of presenting the most serious issues in a humorous and entertaining fashion and so does Sembene. Furthermore, the filmmaker's introduction of musical elements in his works can be compared to the griot's frequent use of songs in his delivery. Sembene favors the use of the Wolof guitar in his soundtrack just as the Senegambian griot likes to accompany himself with that same string instrument.

Structurally, the clear linear progression usually found in Sembene's films can be compared to that of the griot's story. *Mandabi* and *Xala* have the freshness and the atmosphere of tales, while *Emitai* and *Ceddo* reflect the epic tone of some of Africa's oral legends and heroic deeds. Sembene's use of African languages, songs, and proverbs confer on his works the same local flavor which can be found in African storytelling. The circular conversations present in *Emitai* and *Ceddo* are reminiscent of palavers. Then, in traditional tales, " . . . the point of the story is often summed up in a proverb-dicton."[13] This is exactly what happens in *Niaye, Mandabi, Xala,* and *Ceddo.*

In the African oral tradition, the word generally suggests

more than it actually says because the griot makes use of a core of visual imagery and metaphors common to both performer and listener. Sembene's treatment of visual signs adheres to such a principle, and all of his stories can be considered at various levels of meaning beyond their realistic components. Also, it is often noted that his characters are types rather than individuals. They have an overt and a covert significance just as in African storytelling and rituals people are brought to focus more on types represented than the psychological intricacies of the characters.

Sembene's films deal with a world which is well known to his audiences. This trait is also observed in traditional African stories. In his study of the Cameroonian oral tradition, Philip A. Noss observes that "the world of the tale is normally the immediate world of the people for whom it is told. Rarely is the tale about distant places and persons."[14] Because of their familiar context, African oral stories are readily understood by listeners. They present social types like the pauper, the imam, the merchant, and the trickster, all of whom are easily identifiable. The stories also include the king or the princess, legendary forebears known to all. These characters appear in Sembene's films as well. The trickster, for instance, usually a dishonest individual who embodies antisocial traits, appears as the thief or the corrupted civil servant or bourgeois in *Borom Sarret*, *Mandabi*, and *Xala*. The beggars and physically deformed people, who are often a part of African oral stories, are present in Sembene's plots. In *Xala*, the jealous co-wife Oumi and the candid peasant who gets robbed as he comes to town are stock characters of African folklore. The tree which figures in countless African tales and which symbolizes knowledge, life, death, and rebirth or the link between heaven and earth is omnipresent in *Emitai*.

In Sembene's films, people are usually what the viewers see them to be or do on the screen. Except in *Borom Sarret*, *Emitai*, and *Ceddo*, the past of his protagonists is unknown—because of the difference in format in *Black Girl* and *Xala*, the written stories from which they derive often detail their past. Thus, through the immediacy of his typified characters, Sembene reflects collective ideas and attitudes. Soon those protagonists become the parameters of a sociohistorical period, while remaining oral narrative types responding to typical situations. The principal character of *Borom Sarret* has no name and is remembered through his trade and the problems he is not able to overcome. The heroine of *Black Girl* is the victimized black maid rather than Diouana. *Mandabi*'s principal character is the illiterate traditionalist rather than Ibrahima Dieng. *Xala*'s El Hadji Abdoukader Beye is perceived as the unscrupulous impotent businessman and it is as the princess that *Ceddo*'s female protagonist remains in audiences' minds.

Because of religious beliefs widespread in Africa, tales include not only humans and physical objects and landscapes, but also supernatural beings, who, as spirits or ghosts, are made to share the world of the living. In *Emitai*, there is no dividing line between the physical and supernatural worlds as the high priest of the sacred wood communicates directly with the spirits.

Thematic similarities also can be drawn from a comparison between Sembene's films and African tales. Male impotence, which constitutes the basis of *Xala*, is in itself a subject which is often included in the storyteller's repertoire. *Xala*'s theme of punishment of greed, selfishness, vanity, and waste is likewise highly popular in African folktales. So are topics of the lowly rebelling against the powerful and the rescue of the princess, which are both illustrated in *Ceddo*.

In the realm of storytelling, good or bad fortune and curses are very important. This is by no means neglected by Sembene in *Borom Sarret*, where the cart driver's faith in his good fortune results in failure. In *Mandabi*, Dieng hopes that alms giving will favor him. In *Xala*, the main protagonist is the victim of the beggar's vengeful curse.

In many African tales, heroes leave their villages to venture into the unknown, which can be a strange and mysterious forest, an alien land, or extraterrestrial areas inhabited by living spirits or ancestors. The odyssey of such heroes is a quest aimed at the recovery of an object or the finding of their identity. Whether this search is successful varies according to the story, but in most cases it represents an initiatory rite resulting in new knowledge. All these are recurrent elements found in the tales of Birago Diop and Bernard Dadié, which have been directly inspired by African legends.

If the quest for truth of African morality tales is found in storytelling worldwide, the obstacles the protagonist has to overcome and the manner in which this is accomplished essentially reflects African mores. In their archaic initiatory transition from tradition to modernism, as well as through their search for self, most of Sembene's characters also have to face countless obstacles, violated contracts, deceits, and ogre-like unscrupulous individuals. Diouana's journey to a strange land leads her to the land of the dead. The cart driver and Ibrahima Dieng come back to their compound as anti-heroes who have not been able to triumph over the obstacles which hinder their quest in the threatening downtown of Dakar. In the case of *Taw*, the passage to adulthood is at the core of Sembene's plot. Thus, the cure for El Hadji's impotence necessitates cleansing and follows the pattern of death and rebirth common to many African oral stories.

As African tales, Sembene's films not only represent some kind of initiation and metaphorical rebirth, but also cause an initiation, new awareness, and basic change in the existential world view of both the protagonist and the viewer. But if Sembene uses the structure of the African tale, he knows how to adapt it to fit his didactic needs. And, in Mbye B. Cham's words: ". . . Whereas linearity functions in the traditional narrative to underscore the need to preserve and maintain social order and harmony, it works in Sembene's narrative to inspire a struggle against and rejection of unjust social and political order."[15] In Sembene's disenchanted fables, the *prise de conscience* or consciousness awakening of his main character derives from an acute *crise de conscience* or crisis of consciousness brought about by the juxtaposition of opposites in the context within which they evolve: the old versus the new, good versus evil, the weak versus the powerful, poverty versus wealth, and so forth. Henri Agel, undoubtedly influenced by Levi-Strauss's thesis of antagonisms, stressed that such binary oppositions were determinant factors in myths, tales, and poetry and that they were often included in the plot of films.[16] Sembene's motion pictures provide a good example of this observation since the dynamic force of his films relies on a narrative movement between two opposites poles. Thus, one might rightly wonder if the conflicting elements of Sembene's cinematic art are not more related to African oral storytelling rather than solely, as many critics have pointed out, to the Marxist tendencies of his ideology.

By presenting a microcosm of the communities within which they have been created, African oral stories have a pedagogical and social value understood and appreciated by adults as well as children. Tales which include moral codes sanctioned by the society are called morality tales. They constitute the most common and most popular literary genre in black Africa, similar to the European fables and moral tales of the Middle Ages, which also helped people gain a clearer understanding of some aspects of life at a time when literacy was limited. At the same time as they contain moral statements about life and human nature, those tales are social comments on the faults and follies of man, while criticizing some of the social institutions he has established. In that sense, Sembene's films are indeed morality tales, an expression of wisdom, popular belief, and social criticism. Yet Sembene's works, unlike most traditional African stories, are often tales of disenchantment which do not always ensure the successful revenge of the small and the humble against the great and powerful. Neither do they, as a rule, immediately restore an ideal order of justice and benevolence. They do, however, suggest or advocate their implementation. Moreover, Sembene's motion pictures derive specifically from African dilemma tales, the outcome of which is debated and in a way decided by the spectators. With the open-endedness of most of his plots, Sembene trusts the viewers' imagination to prolong his films. in *Borom Sarret, Mandabi*, and *Ceddo*, he leaves his spectators with a choice between several alternatives as the film comes to a close.

In addition to being compared to tales, the works of Ousmane Sembene also show similarities with Africa's ancient and modern drama, both of which have developed from the oral tradition. Sembene's films can be compared in some respects with traditional Yoruba theater or the Ikaki masquerade. Like traditional African drama, they include satirical comedies and historical re-enactments. Similarly, they use largely nonprofessional actors from the community they intend to reach and have the "plot unity" of traditional African drama. The following quote by Bakary Traoré on Mandingo theater could be applied almost in its entirety to Sembene's cinema, whose purpose is to generate or maintain ethical values: " . . . the essential function of the Kote Komanyaga of the Mandingo theatre is to make a public spectacle of all efforts to violate the group's moral code: conjugal infidelity, theft, jealousy, etc. . . . and thereby ensure their suppression. . . . "[17]

Sembene's works also offer similarities with modern African drama, inspired by traditional African and European theater. *Xala* calls to mind Nigerian dramatist J. P. Clark's 1966 *Song of a Goat* in which the male protagonist has lost his virility, allegedly because of an ancestral curse. The tone of *Mandabi* is reminiscent of G. Oyono Mbia's social comedies. Sembene's protagonists in *Emitai* and *Ceddo* speak sometimes in proverbs in the same style as Nigerian playwright Wole Soyinka's characters often do. In the same manner, both authors' heroes have very specific social roles. Sembene and Soyinka, as well as numerous other African authors use their art to reflect the world around them and influence it. They focus on the social patterns and the political events of present-day Africa caught between tradition and modernism. While written literature is unknown to the bulk of African people, Sembene's cinema, like African drama, is more accessible to them. It can indeed be compared to African theater since "perhaps the most important thing to stress is that theatre is being used in Africa as a means of education, celebration, protest and discovery."[18]

Although identical structures and intentions exist between Sembene's films and African storytelling as well as drama, there are also limits to such a comparison. If in Africa the collective experience of watching movies reminds one of the audience attending the griot's delivery, films remain the same each time they are presented. They do not have the improvisatory nature, the flexibility, and the versatility of the oral transmitter. The griot can, at any time, respond to the audience's reaction by altering his tone of voice, by introducing new gestures, mimes, and repetitions, and by interpolating songs. Films do not allow such emotional and lyrical interaction of the teller and listener. Furthermore, film screening usually takes place in an enclosed room which does not offer the vivacious communal appeal of the village square or the nocturnal atmosphere of evening gatherings in African compounds, which is so propitious to the magic of storytelling. Films can be seen casually and on an everyday basis, whereas some griots perform only on the occasion of cyclical festivals and special celebrations.

"The traditional story-teller no longer exists today and I think that the filmmaker can replace him," says Sembene.[19] These words—stressing the important role of the African filmmaker—should not be taken literally. The griot is still very much a part of African culture even if he lacks the unchallenged appeal he once had in all of Africa. Admittedly, oral tradition is progressively disappearing in Africa's changing societies because of the expansion of education and modern mass media such as radio, television, and cinema. Nevertheless, it could be argued that African filmmaking and the works of Sembene in particular make use of or expand storytelling rather than supplant it. Not only do Sembene's films evolve from storytelling, but they also preserve it. As writer Bernard Dadié once said: "We have treasures to convey: our message must be transmitted, we will do so in expressing our values under new forms."[20] Sembene's cinema undeniably stands proud among such new forms.

According to many authors, tales have nourished most written literary genres in black African culture. Such contemporary writers as Birago Diop (Senegal) and Bernard Dadié (Ivory Coast) have produced written versions of traditional stories—as did the brothers Grimm in nineteenth-century Europe—or they have used them as a basis for new ones. Likewise, the influence of oral tradition can hardly be missed in the novels of Mongo Beti (Cameroon), Aminata Sow Fall (Senegal), or Ousmane Sembene himself. As a writer, Sembene recognizes having been influenced by the griot.[21] As he transfers his talents from writing to filmmaking, Sembene remains faithful to the same source of inspiration: African oral tradition. He is not remote from his people, creating works limited to the intelligentsia. Instead, he continues the role of the griot as the chronicler of his people's history. According to Mbye B. Cham, Sembene is "a blend of the most relevant, useful and progressive aspects of both the 'gewel' and the 'lebkat.' "[22] He is the kind of griot who has maintained an almost complete freedom of expression and should not be confused with the court griot owing allegiance to a powerful family or group. Sembene's objective is not to provide an escape from reality by embellishing it, for "the griot may only embellish reality during victorious times through what people call court songs or festive songs. In times of crisis, however, a griot does not embellish reality. On the contrary, he finds himself in the brutality of surrounding events. I have never·tried to please my audiences through the embellishment of reality. I am a participant and an observer of my society."[23]

The constant social criticism present in Sembene's films attests to the fact that his has remained a free and independent spirit. As a subversive artist he is often censored and kept apart from the mainstream of society like the *griot casté*, the slave without master, who, at the same time as he is considered an important transmitter of culture is paradoxically shunned as a helot. "The African filmmaker is like the griot who is similar to the European minstrel: a man of learning and common sense who is the historian, the raconteur, the living memory and the conscience of his people."[24]

It is as a griot that Sembene uses the magical, emotional, and mystical aspect of film experience to create new depths of understanding. For Sembene, "the African filmmaker is the griot of modern times."[25] It is as such that he defines himself, saying: "I am a storyteller and I tell stories. I hope to tell more of them and better ones."[26]

NOTES

1. Ousmane Sembene, "Filmmakers and African Culture," *Africa* n. 71 (1977), p. 80.
2. Georges Balandier and Jacques Maquet, *Dictionary of Black African Civilization* (New York: Léon Amiel, 1974), p. 161.

3. Ibid.
4. Elolongué Epanya Yondo, *La Place de la Littérature Orale en Afrique* (Paris: La Pensée Universelle, 1976), p. 101.
5. Dorothy S. Blair, translator, *Birago Diop's Tales of Amadou Koumba* (London: Oxford University Press, 1966), p. ix.
6. Mbye B. Cham, "Oral Narrative Patterns in the Work of Ousmane Sembene," unpublished paper (1982), p. 4.
7. Elolongué Epanya Yondo, *La Place de la Littérature Orale en Afrique*, p. 23. Author's translation.
8. Ibid.
9. Alphonse Raphaël N'Diaye, "Les Traditions Orales et la Quête de l'Identité Culturelle," *Présence Africaine*, n. 114 (1980), p. 9. Author's translation.
10. Joseph M. Boggs, *The Art of Watching Films* (Menlo Park, Calif.: Benjamin/Cummings Publishing Co., 1978), p. 19.
11. Haile Gerima at the symposium "Literature, Film and Society in Africa: Dialectics of Artistic Creativity and Social Consciousness," organized by the African Studies Program at the University of Illinois, Urbana-Champaign, May 1–3, 1980.
12. Michel Capdenac, "Le Mandat, film sénégalais de Sembene Ousmane," *Les Lettres Françaises*, n. 1259 (1968), p. 22. Author's translation.
13. Joyce A. Hutchinson, ed., *Birago Diop—Contes Choisis* (Cambridge: Cambridge University Press, 1967), p. 15.
14. Philip A. Noss in Daniel J. Crowley, ed., *African Folklore in the New World* (Austin: University of Texas Press, 1977), p. 86.
15. Mbye B. Cham, "Oral Narrative Patterns in the Work of Ousmane Sembene," p. 6.
16. Henri Agel, *Métaphysique du Cinéma* (Paris: Payot, 1976), pp. 197–206.
17. Bakary Traoré, *The Black African Theater and Its Social Functions* (Ibadan, Nigeria: Ibadan University Press, 1972), p. 66.
18. Martin Banham with Clive Wake, *African Theater Today* (London: Pitman Publishing, 1976), p. v.
19. Noureddine Ghali, "Ousmane Sembene," *Cinéma 76*, n. 208 (1976), p. 89. Author's translation.
20. Joyce A. Hutchinson, ed., *Birago Diop—Contes Choisis*, p. 8. Author's translation.
21. Ousmane Sembene, *L'Harmattan* (Paris: Présence Africaine, 1963), p. 9.
22. Mbye B. Cham, "Oral Narrative Patterns in the Work of Ousmane Sembene," p. 4.

23. From a series of interviews with Ousmane Sembene conducted by the author in Senegal in 1978.

24. Françoise Pfaff, "Notes on Cinema," *New Directions*, vol. 6, n. 1 (1979), p. 26.

25. From a lecture delivered by Ousmane Sembene at Howard University, Washington, D.C., 19 February 1978.

26. Sembene to author, Senegal, 1978.

3
THE AFRICANNESS OF SEMBENE'S FILM LANGUAGE

REALISM

"We have had enough of feathers and tom-toms," declares Sembene, alluding to the way in which Africa has been described by many non-African directors who would rather show cheap exoticism than tackle themes of Africa's historical and social reality.[1] For Sembene, society is a dynamic whole and film is but its reflector. So, from his first film, it is precisely such a reality that he has chosen to portray. As he writes the plot for his films, Sembene draws his inspiration from true historical facts (*Emitai, Ceddo*) or actual events. *Niaye* illustrates "a case of incest which actually took place and the young girl had to leave her village."[2] *Black Girl* emerged from the suicide of a black maid which was reported in the current event column of *Nice-Matin*, a French newspaper shown in the film.[3] About *Xala*, the filmmaker specifies, "according to some people the 'xala'—or spell of impotence—does exist."[4]

Yet if films are based on reality how can such a reality be completely transferred to the screen? The controversy concerning the nature of cinema in its relationship with reality is as old as cinema itself: Louis Lumiére was, at first, chiefly interested in recording daily events in a natural setting but at the same time, another pioneer of early French cinema, Mélies, became immediately involved in the enormous manipulative potential of film to transform reality.

Nowadays, most film theorists believe that though film may be the privileged medium of reality, it is also an art. As such, it goes beyond a mere mechanical reproduction of reality through the use of cameras and projectors. In film, the elements of reality are rearranged according to the possibilities and limitations of that medium: the film process and the flatness and two-dimensional aspect of film image as opposed to the three dimensionality of real bodies and objects, which do not appear on the screen in their true proportion but appear distorted in perspective. They are perceived according to the viewer's accuracy of vision. This perception is itself limited to a particular optical spectrum. Thus, film image is limited by its frame and can present only a section of real life. Film, as a window on reality, excludes as well as includes parts of an entity it does not completely represent but may suggest or symbolize. In effect, cinema does not transmit reality. Rather, through the mental activity of both the director and the audience and physical resources it provides, through what once was aptly named a magic lantern, an illusion of reality. Using the objectivity of technique as well as the subjectivity of the director's point of view, film reproduces, reshapes, and reconstructs actual facts into a new reality which may be close to objective reality. Realism, thus, can be only an artistic representation or selection of a reality inherently different from true reality. In all cases, film is fiction derived from the director's artistic vision based on his or her culture and philosophical and ideological patterns. This fiction is intelligible to the viewer because the filmmaker has adapted it to the viewer's visual and aural perception through a series of signs and symbols identifiable by both.

Independent filmmakers like Sembene do not have to "endure" the dictates of the producers of big film studios and thus may be freer than others to choose the distance they want to establish between reality and its cinematic representation. They may wish for the visual accuracy of their material to fit their pattern of thoughts. In his literary works, Sembene has realistically depicted characters caught up in the political, social, and economic reality of Senegal at various stages of its history. Except for some poetry, most of his writings are in prose and propose a sociorealistic view of his environment with a marked sympathy for the deprived and the oppressed with whom he empathizes on a number of social issues. In investigating Sembene's film language, it would be interesting to find out whether he has retained in his cinematic works the same realistic approach as in his written works.

Defining Sembene's film language is greatly facilitated by the fact that he is, as scriptwriter, producer, director, and editor, the dominant creative force of his films. Although all of his films are a cooperative effort, Sembene can certainly be considered as their primary unifying force since he is responsible for the majority of the creative decisions affecting them. Thus, having assessed the importance of the director's input and control in the definition of Sembene's aesthetics, one has now to determine how and why the filmmaker selects and represents the raw material he extracts from actual facts.

Since film presents only a fragmented view of a given reality, selected by its author to fit a particular purpose, the film images derive from the selection the director makes from real life. In *Emitai*, Sembene, opposed to excessive violence on the screen, excludes the actual massacre of the whole village by French troops. In his own words: "*Emitai* is based on a true story, but the film does not illustrate the total historical truth since the village was raided and its inhabitants massacred."[5] Then it is only to link the effects of French presence in Senegal to those in the Maghrib that the filmmaker includes a "legionnaire" in his story. Historically, the legion has never fought or been stationed in Senegal, while it did fight in North Africa.

However realistic Sembene's portrayals of women are throughout his films, they are limited to certain segments of the Senegalese female population and do not include certain socioprofessional categories such as seasonal women, that is, the migrant workers from rural areas who come to the city to face a most uncertain future. He does not depict factory workers, professional women, career women, or artists. Furthermore, he does not allude to a number of issues related to women in Senegal (prostitution, excision, the ostracism of the sterile woman, infanticide, and others). Nor does he show all the varied roles of women in Senegalese society (religion, initiatory ceremonies). Sembene's purpose in making films is not to compose sociological or anthropological documentaries that would cover all the issues related to Senegalese women. He attempts to convey an artistic view of a selected reality comprising female characters.

Since filmmaking also involves a transformation and a displacement of reality, Sembene sometimes chooses to "stage" reality, as happens in *Ceddo* during a scene in which people undergo a conversion to Islam rendered in a most dramatic and impressive fashion. Here the reality of historical truth is restructured to provoke stimulus in the viewer's mind.

In addition to the director's artistic vision and choices, the degree of realism in what is finally shown in films is also determined by financial factors. In *Ceddo*, for instance, the historical accuracy and detail of the workings of the king's court might have benefited from a higher budgetary allocation.

Apart from economic considerations, the "realism" of a film also may be affected by the controlling political forces behind it. In Senegal as well as in many other countries, those forces, which Sembene vindictively calls "the inquisition," have an effect upon the decisions made by the censors to exclude from a given film scenes emphasizing a physical and/or symbolic reality they wish to hide (when the film is not entirely banned).[6] For this reason, a scene of *Xala* in which a white police chief clears Dakar of its beggars in a rather harsh manner has yet to be shown. This scene was censored in Senegal, where the police superintendent at that time was French. Another scene likewise cut is that in which the beggar tells Awa, who wants to summon the police, that people in jail are happier than workers and peasants because they are fed and receive some care.[7] *Xala* underwent a total of ten cuts. When this film was released in Senegal, Sembene offset such censorship by distributing leaflets explaining which scenes had been removed from the film. Then, in order to shoot on location, Senegalese filmmakers must also obtain a permit from the government. According to Sembene, this law is strictly enforced. It limits his freedom of action as it does for other filmmakers since, here again, such measures are applied in many countries and may shape the content of a given fictional reality.

In Senegal, Sembene's approach to reality through his films has brought a dualistic response from his compatriots. Those opposed to the regime presently in power find his sociorealism and social criticism sugar coated and argue that the political tensions of Senegal are dissolved in lyrical and/or comic sequences. Proponents of that same regime contend that Sembene's attack on the new Senegalese elite is too severe and that he is exploiting poverty, distress, and corruption for the sake of sensationalism, creating an unfavorable image of his country. Such feelings are reflected in the following excerpt from an interview conducted in 1978 with Assane Seck, then Minister of Culture:

In the last scene of *Xala*, people spit on El Hadji. Well, such a scene does not exist in reality. It cannot exist. One day, when I was Minister of Foreign Affairs, Senegalese ambassadors gathered and we showed *Xala*. Sembene was with us. Our ambassadors were embarrassed when the film, with its army of beggars, was shown abroad. Sembene was asked where he had seen this. He answered: "it does not exist." We asked him where he had seen people spitting as is the case in *Xala*. He answered the same thing. But, he countered, in Senegal, when something disgusts us deeply, we draw the spit from the depths of our throats and we throw it sideways, far away. This is true. The idea is true but the fact that this is done to someone, as it occurs in *Xala*, is inaccurate. . . . The act is symbolic. People strive to understand what they see. This is why some of our films are successful in Senegal and not abroad. There, they are not understood. . . . Using images which do not exist in reality . . . can mislead people.[8]

In Senegal, if Sembene's films always raise popular interest, they are also frequently met with a lack of official enthusiasm. Yet Sembene is still able to obtain financial support from his government which attests to liberalism in Senegalese cultural policies. It should be stressed that this liberalism is absent in many other developing countries when filmmakers treat political themes.

Sembene's films reflect his concern for the poor for whom he advocates change and equity. However, his films show a definite partiality to the fate of the impoverished and fail to mention that there is, indeed, some work of social improvement taking place in Senegal.

SPACE AND TIME

In rearranging space and time, African filmmakers underscore their preference for a linear narrative mode, long sequences, a minimal discontinuity in time, and the reflection of a physical and social space which incorporates man in his entirety (according to animistic and holistic views) and in symbiosis with his milieu—thus, one notes a greater number of medium shots as opposed to close-ups and a propensity to use long shots and limited camera movement.

The "pictureness" of Sembene's films does not appear to fit closely any set of rules. Yet his approach to space and time reveals similarities to those mentioned above for the simple reason that many African filmmakers were influenced by Sembene and because they all work in the same context. Striving for realism, Sembene adheres primarily to a realistic/naturalistic approach to space in his films. He chiefly uses partially organized outdoor natural locations and shoots inside sparingly and only when necessary. This may be explained by limited budgets and a wish to eliminate the cost as well as the technical complexities of indoor lighting, since African cinema is still hampered by a lack of film technicians. It can also be assumed that Sembene wishes to recreate African life which, because of weather, agricultural structures, and communal activities, takes place outside (*Niaye, Emitai, Ceddo*). Enclosed spaces, however, are handled by Sembene in *Mandabi* and *Xala* to reflect the intricacies of modern administration and business or the bareness, sterility, and sparse furnishing of many homes of the Senegalese nouveaux riches. Sembene's representation of the environment often suggests an interpretation of the role of the environment in the formation of his characters. In his settings are found clues that facilitate the understanding of the characters and their function in the story (as is the case in *Mandabi* and *Xala*). *Borom Sarret* is often photographed in long and low angle shots which reduce the stature of the principal character and accentuate the size of buildings as well as the stony brutality of the city. Sembene's use of space as he follows the cartman downtown underscores his personal unimportance and his subjection to outside forces. The same observation holds true for Dieng in *Mandabi*. Dieng's move from the city's outskirts to its inner bureaucratic sanctum is seen on eye level and his itinerary appears as less desperate than that of Pudovkin's peasant in *The End of St. Petersburg* (1927), whose dwarf-sized perspective accentuates the inhuman might of the city and his own vulnerability. For Sembene, realism does not exclude symbolism, as evidenced in *Xala* where the Chamber of Commerce not only represents the location but a multitude of ideas associated with such a place. Likewise in *Xala*, the beggars' march to the city is perceived in the manner of Eisenstein in long shot, middle distance, and from varied angles to stress their unflinching determination and the symbolic aspect of their return and repossession of spaces from which they were evicted. *Borom Sarret*'s unsuccessful journey to the center of the city as well as Dieng's hallucinatory "to-and-fro motion" to downtown Dakar reflect Sembene's perception of space as a delimitation of physically contrasted social spheres to which his characters belong. This passage from one sphere to another raises a series of obstacles and ends in failure as a possible reflection of Senegal's static and rigid class/caste system. Dieng's attempt to cross social spaces reminds one of a similar wandering of the unemployed found in *Bicycle Thief* (1948). In both cases, the protagonists' quests lead back to the city's periphery, a marginal world from which it is hard to escape.

If in Sembene's films a motion within space from outward to inward is hampered, the reverse is no easier. El Hadji, who is now used to his air-conditioned surroundings and Mercedes, finds it physically almost unbearable to ride a cart on the jerking dirt road leading to a marabout's village. In *Black Girl*, as Diouana's former employer crosses the narrow bridge to Diouana's neighborhood, his passage to the "other world"/ "underworld" appears threatening and perilous. Those considerations should not suggest that Sembene's overall message is pessimistic. If there is any rapport between character and landscape, his pictures of rivers (*Emitai*) and bustling streets (*Borom Sarret, Mandabi*) with traffic moving upwards within the frame infer dynamism and change. Moreover, the return of Borom Sarret and Dieng to the confining space of their compound is not an end in itself. Their prostration is compensated by the movement of others around them who move outside of that space and who provide possible solutions to the entrapment of the characters.

In most of his films, Sembene emphasizes communal space rather than individual space due to the collective aspect of traditional African life as well as his own ideology, which stresses the importance of social action. It is significant that in films about rural areas, Sembene favors long shots, panoramic shots, and eye-level shots, while in urban settings he uses more close-ups, medium shots, and more sophisticated camera and lens movement, as well as contrasting shots with varied angles to delineate his protagonists' conflicts in unfamiliar surroundings. Here again, instead of elaborate dollies, Sembene uses the element present in the environment to create specific effects and a particular symbolic meaning as happens in the downward shot, usually related to forthcoming danger, taken from a caged elevator as Diouana comes down after her first fruitless search for a job. Sembene's camera movements are not elaborate and perhaps he is in agreement with John Ford, who contended that camera movement destroys reality. Sembene likes to shoot his pictures with natural frames like the feet of Borom Sarret framing the crawling beggar's face seen from a high angle, or the multiple doors within which Dieng is literally and symbolically "framed" in *Mandabi*.

Another spatial distinction made by Sembene in most of his motion pictures is that of sacred space versus secular space. Many of his characters evolve between sacred spaces—represented by a prayer circle (*Borom Sarret, Mandabi, Ceddo*), a mosque (*Borom Sarret, Mandabi*), a sacred forest (*Emitai, Ceddo*), or the marabouts' compound (*Xala*)—and the open space of the country or the city (for example, *Borom Sarret,*

Mandabi, Emitai, and *Ceddo*). Generally, Sembene's characters seek comfort, relief, or hope in a sacred space in communion with the divine. These forces are expected to resolve the crisis faced in the profane physical world. Protected and functioning momentarily in their sacred spaces, these protagonists become helpless and lost in the real world. Here Sembene comments on the escapist characteristics in beliefs which propose religious stability as a remedy for a chaotic universe. The characters' domestic space, furthermore, reflects security, in sharp contrast with their vulnerability in a more extended context (in *Borom Sarret, Mandabi,* and to some extent in *Xala*). Finally, Sembene frequently uses the dramatic tension provided by two divergent social spaces as happens when he contrasts El Hadji's marriage feast to the sharing of the beggars' meager supply of food. "Unlike real life, film permits to jump in time and space. Montage means joining together shots of situations that occur at different times and in different places."[9] The manipulation of time by a director and the overall combination of different shots gives a particular pulse to a film. Some critics have said that the rhythm of Sembene's films is generally slower than that of many Western films because of his use of long takes adapted to the continuity of his narrative and his wish for his films to remain as close as possible to the real time of the story. Such assumptions only apply to his works dealing with rural milieus or those translated in a lyrical mood. A frame-by-frame analysis of *Xala*, for instance, reveals that the takes of this film are much shorter than those of *Emitai* or *Ceddo* and are more comparable in length to those of Western films. For a more realistic rendering of his stories, Sembene adapts the tempo of his film to the story he narrates. He makes no use of either slow, accelerated, or backward motion because, in this area as well, he wants to retain as much naturalness as possible.

Showing concern for the clarity of his stories, which have to be understood even by the most cinematically unsophisticated audiences, Sembene avoids visual ambiguity and a confusing cross-cutting of events that are disconnected from each other in space as well as in time. His are usually clear-cut stories in which a human fate serves as a statement of universal significance. Whenever possible, he respects the linear pattern of his narration in order not to disrupt the natural unity of his plot. But since the format of film does not allow a perfect matching between the time of the story and the time of the narrative, he occasionally uses, to include appropriate information, flashbacks (*Black Girl*), flash forwards (*Ceddo*), dream sequences (*Ceddo*), dream sequences/flashbacks (*Mandabi, Taw*), and parallel time (*Ceddo*). Asked once why he does not make greater use of flashbacks, Sembene simply answered: "Because the themes of my films do not require it."[10] To achieve a better connection between his films and the culture from which they derive Sembene utilizes slow seasonal time, like the sowing, harvesting, and rice storing of *Emitai*, which regulates the pace of life in rural Africa. Sembene stresses that "this pacing rhythm reflects my own life. I am presenting our own cultural style, which does not have the same rapidity or quickness as the style of Afro-American society. It is here that you have to accept and recognize that mine is a completely different world. I could make a quick film, with rapid montage, but it would not be true to our society. I am making films for my own country."[11] The daily cyclical time of prayers and rituals is observed as well in *Borom Sarret, Mandabi*, and *Ceddo* and generates the illusion of a mythical, stable present.

On three occasions, at the end of *Black Girl, Xala*, and *Ceddo*, Sembene chooses to fix both time and space in a freeze frame, whose startling effect emphasizes the inconclusiveness of the plots by delaying their resolution beyond the last picture. As in Truffaut's *400 Blows* (1959), Diouana's little brother's steady gaze at the viewers forces them to look within themselves for an answer to the boy's dilemma. More than the indeterminacy usually linked to such process, Sembene's freeze frame invites the viewers to find their own conclusion beyond the confines of the story or in their immediate reality.

ACTORS

To interpret their characters so that they remain as close as possible to reality, some directors (like the Italian neo-realists) have elected to use non-professional actors, preferably coming from the same sociocultural background as their characters. This has, until now, been Sembene's choice. Except for Robert Fontaine, a French theater actor (in both *Black Girl* and *Emitai*), and Douta Seck, a Senegalese actor (in *Xala*), Sembene has not used any other experienced actors in his films. Insisting on the naturalistic aspect of his motion pictures, he works very efficiently with his non-professional actors so that they don't "act" but rather keep their usual mannerisms and language (except in his early films in French co-produced with France) as well as all the visible characteristics for which he has selected them. They are neither made to talk nor gesticulate more than they would in reality, for Sembene knows that too much emphasis given to the verbal aspect of films distracts the audience from the story which may then become unnatural and stylized, as happens in *Ceddo*. He also uses nonprofessional actors because their personalities provide an easier identification with common people. "Professional actors are simply not convincing as laborers, as ordinary human beings. Of course, if the story seems right, . . . I might consider using professional actors one day. They do make wonderful gangsters and dead kings."[12]

There are, in fact, only a few professional actors in Senegal. Those have mostly been trained at the Dakar School of Fine Arts. According to Sembene, "acting is not considered a profession in Senegal. The beautiful young woman in *Black Girl* is still a seamstress, although she recently went to Moscow to play Mrs. Lumumba in a film. And Mamadou Guye [*sic*], who was so marvelous as the hero of *Mandabi*, was discovered working behind a desk in a tiny office at an airline company. He's still sitting behind that desk."[13] Sembene also finds working with Senegalese actors difficult:

It often happens that many actors from the School of Fine Arts who worked with us had to be retrained. . . . These actors are the ones who are most saturated with Western culture. The school trained them in all the classic plays of seventeenth-century French theater. Therefore, one has to erase all their training and return them to their social environment. Meanwhile, there is no such problem with nonprofessional actors. They are somewhat the role they play, the way they believe, and everything else.[14]

Although Sembene's non-professional actors are left some freedom to improvise, they have to undergo several rehearsals because the small budget of Sembene's films and the immediate unavailability of rushes generally limits his shooting ability to one take. Sembene explains: "I work with the actors before shooting. There are two things to consider: I can improvise, so can the actors. We have an outline on which we agreed and at a given time we have to improvise because we don't want to work in a studio. I work a lot outside. It's open-air cinema."[15]

A lot of the non-professional actors of *Emitai* were soldiers who had fought on the other side of Senegal's border for the independence of their country, Guinea-Bissau, from Portuguese colonialism. Sembene could have limited his choice of actors to the Casamance villagers but instead asked for Cabral's agreement to use his freedom fighters, thus creating a symbolic link between *Emitai*'s struggle against colonialism and theirs.

Sembene's direction of non-professional actors is usually good and convincing. Sometimes, specific preparations and negotiations may be involved to obtain the cooperation of villagers. This happened in *Emitai*.

> You have to be in the environment for a certain period of time so that you get used to the people and the environment. In turn, the people have to get used to you. Customarily, I explain to them what I want to do and why I want to do it. I go to see the village chief. I negotiate and I discuss with him. I bring some film, I take a few shots and then we talk everything over. Money and/or gifts play an important role in these negotiations. . . . Then, when the shooting is over, the villagers come to get their salary.[16]

As he used non-professional actors in *Emitai*, Sembene had members of the actual village council play their own role in the film and they were allowed to improvise their verbal interventions. Also respecting the customs adapted to the villagers' sociocultural milieu, he filmed *Emitai* during the growing season while they were not involved in land care or harvest. Essentially, Sembene uses film to transmit a particular message to specific audiences. It is therefore important in his stories that the characters should not be overshadowed by the personality of the actor. The viewer's attention should go to the film itself rather than to a star whose personality pre-exists that of the character he embodies. By employing non-professional actors, Sembene does not have to face this competition between actor and character and retains full control over the characterization and acting process of his films. At the same time, he remains faithful to traditional African performance in which non-professional actors and dancers are taken directly from the community. Often wearing masks, those actors subordinate their physical and psychological personalities to the roles they play. Thus, at African festivals, spectators are accustomed to an aesthetic distance with the performer and do not focus as much on the personality of the actor as on that of the types or roles he plays. In addition, the star system used by Hollywood to ensure the success of its high budget films is based on their audiences' psychological need for the predictable, the comfortable, and the reassuring. This is fulfilled whenever familiar faces and personalities are seen. This is totally opposed to Sembene's aim in making films. He does not want to comfort his viewers but rather disquiet them. He prefers to induce reflection through an identification process greatly facilitated by anonymous non-professional actors (taken from their own surroundings) rather than dreamlike glamorous stars.

Usually, Sembene works with different groups of people for each of his films. However, it sometimes happens that he uses the same individual in several of his motion pictures: Robert Fontaine appears as the French commander in *Emitai* and as Diouana's employer in *Black Girl* to emphasize the link between French colonialism and neo-colonialism in Senegal. Makhourédia Gueye was used three times by Sembene; as Dieng in *Mandabi*, as the president of the Chamber of Commerce in *Xala*, and as the king in *Ceddo*. Here a parallel can be drawn between the king who accepts the intrusion of Islamic imperialism and the president of the Chamber of Commerce who is a tool of French neo-colonialism in independent Senegal. Sembene likes to emphasize that the adolescent who leads the beggars in *Xala* is the same one who played Diouana's little brother in *Black Girl*. He does this to point out that a character who, at the end of *Black Girl*, was the bearer of many hopes is in *Xala* (made nine years later) fearlessly leading the march of the dispossessed.

Not only does Sembene write and direct his films, but he also occasionally performs in them as well. In such instances, he manipulates reality on two levels and espouses the function of the Spanish *autores* who, in medieval theater, used to be both actors and heads of troupes (not to mention Shakespeare or Molière). Sembene plays the role of the schoolmaster in *Black Girl*, the public writer of *Mandabi*, and the black soldier who makes fun of French military institutions in *Emitai*. In *Ceddo*, he is featured as one of the rebellious villagers. Questioned about the similarities between the roles he interprets and his own personality, he denies having consciously selected them for that reason. Yet it is striking that Sembene, an advocate of film as a means of education, plays the role of schoolmaster in *Black Girl*, a character on the edge of tradition and modernity, able to record and to teach the events he has witnessed. Likewise, as a socially inclined writer before becoming a filmmaker, Sembene interprets the role of the "public" writer. Then, having served in the French colonial army, he is one of *Emitai*'s African soldiers. Finally, in real life the owner of a house called "Galle Ceddo" (the house of the Ceddo), Sembene precisely elects to interpret the part of cne Ceddo in his latest film to date. Sembene clarifies the brief appearances he sporadically makes in his films as follows:

> I kind of like playing in my films, but I do not play roles that are purposely interrelated throughout my works or connected to my personality or my own experience. . . . Pragmatically, my playing in my films encourages the non-professional actors because at the beginning, people used to identify actors with the griots who are people of low caste. In *Ceddo*, I was asking people who had been taking care of their hair for years to shave their head. So I decided to become a Ceddo myself and to have my head shaved to show solidarity with the actors. This is part of my method of work: people understand that I am not the boss but that I participate.[17]

Sembene's acting in his own films does not at all have the dominating presence of Orson Welles. Neither are Sembene's roles as an occasional actor casual appearances like those of Hitchcock, who always remains at the periphery of the action. Sembene claims that his participation is for purely pragmatic reasons and discards any further comparison with the British master of suspense, abruptly stating: "It is not Hitchcock's way, it is Sembene's way."[18]

OBJECTS AND THEIR SYMBOLISM

In their expression of reality, filmmakers employ objects as cultural codes for what they reflect and what they imply. Besides actors, objects are what makes fictional reality understood by viewers. They force them to go beyond the image of the object to the meaning of the object in film fiction and reality.

Objects have both obvious and hidden meanings. They have an explicit and implicit value according to the associations of images, ideas, responses, and feelings they generate, consciously or unconsciously, in the mind of the filmmaker and the viewers. In Senegal, objects are sometimes believed to have a life of their own (animism) and what is called "art" is often more symbolic than realistic. In such a context, Sembene's use of objects can scarcely be coincidental but is rather the result of a careful choice. He explains his handling of objects as follows: "Generally, I use certain objects as sociocultural and historical reference marks. Film language requires a certain punctuation and some objects allow me to punctuate my films."[19]

Objects must fit the social environment shown on the screen except when some special effects are sought. The power of objects to create a world is exploited in *Ceddo*, where the *samp* (challenge stick) repeatedly symbolizes the bravery and honor of Wolof knighthood. At the beginning of *Emitai*, the close-up of a fallen spear as the owner is captured announces to the viewer the Diola's impending defeat. This image is strongly associated with the medium shot of an adolescent's ritualistic dance with a gun at the end of the film. It suggests that in the future such wars for freedom will be won only with similar weaponry and a technology equal to that of the adversary. According to Sembene, "the samp is a stick which symbolized challenge a long time ago at the time when the film takes place. It means that someone had to challenge someone else to repair a wrongdoing. Then, a confrontation (a war or a fight) would ensue. Now it is mainly among wrestlers that those rules are to be found."[20]

Not only the nature of objects, but their place, movement, size, and importance in relation to their environment can be manipulated by the filmmaker to guide the audience's attention. They can be made more or less conspicuous due to the manner in which they are shown. In close-ups, more importance is given to certain objects which are thus isolated from their environment. At the same time, they are also symbols of that environment which they partly reflect. Such happens with Sembene's representation of various traditional African objects each time he wishes to establish a reference to African authenticity. In *Black Girl* and *Emitai*, traditional masks fill the screen on several occasions. In *Xala*, one sees the top of the beggar's stick, an African face, which goes, seemingly moving by itself, from one end of the screen to the other. A subsequent picture reveals that only the top of the stick was shot and that its motion was due to the beggar's carrying it like a sceptre or a *samp*. The isolated motion given to this object draws attention. Then, its link with Africanness and its suggested comparison with a sceptre or samp lend the beggar's stick, and the beggar himself, a higher symbolic value (that is, challenge) than it might have had as a simple walking stick. In other cases, Sembene separates a traditional object from its usual function to condemn the cultural alienation of a particular group of people. The African mask which is passed around among the members of the Chamber of Commerce in *Xala* to gather the votes about El Hadji's dismissal has lost the meaning for which it was intended. It stresses the cultural alienation of the Senegalese nouveaux riches whose mercantile greed shows no respect for their ancestors' sacred beliefs.

The supernatural qualities of ceremonial objects are depicted in the scenes of the sacred wood of *Emitai* and in *Xala* during the visit El Hadji makes to a village marabout. Sembene uses the resources of the film process and the "magic" of cinema to make objects as well as people disappear at will. This occurs in the sequence during which the Diola address their gods. The supernatural properties of amulets are better understood as they "disappear" while handled by El Hadji's marabout. Such disappearances of objects would usually be exploited by Western filmmakers for comical or surrealistic effects. In Sembene's African frame of reference, they relate to the supernatural ambiance of religious beliefs deeply ingrained in people's minds and life-styles.

In Sembene's motion pictures, amulets, which are at once familiar and invested with a spiritual significance, function as unifying elements. In all of his films, for instance, he shows characters with amulets to emphasize the presence of traditional African religion at all levels of Senegalese society despite Islamic or Catholic influence. He emphasizes that "people talk incessantly about the power of amulets. . . . One has to see how Senegalese people ritually touch their forearms, waist, or feet to feel their *gris gris*. . . . Representatives, secretaries of state, and even presidents in Africa may have their individual witch doctors. We are in a period of insecurity and people in power call upon everybody and everything as they call on the army."[21] Throughout *Xala*, which a critic describes as a "masquerade in Dakar," a comedy of possession/dispossession based on appearance, costumes, and pretense, Sembene denounces with acerbity the new imported fetishes of Senegal's elite: cars, wigs, attaché cases (one is even carried by El Hadji to his own wedding), suits, air-conditioning units, sunglasses, green lawns, American soda, French mineral water, and champagne.[22] Those are rejected by El Hadji as he is evicted by his peers when he suddenly praises the "real" power of "true fetishes." In *Xala*, the Mercedes and other imported luxury cars occupy a special place in Sembene's iconography. They symbolize the apparent power and class solidarity of the businessmen as they slowly drive away, one by one in a pompous parade, to go to El Hadji's wedding. Usually, these imported cars are carefully shot from various distances and angles by Sembene, who, through them, demonstrates the businessmen's cultural and economic dependency. A little girl's white doll in *Mandabi* and the white groom and bride dolls of El Hadji's wedding cake bear similar connotations.

In a manner reminiscent of early Soviet cinema, similar to Pudovkin's handling of statues rather than Eisenstein's omnipotent mechanical visual symbolism, Sembene makes use of statues to underline sociocultural anachronisms. As young Senegalese are being enrolled by force in the French Army, the insert of a statue of a white soldier holding a black soldier by his shoulders in a most friendly fashion stresses the gap existing between the facts of history and their official French memorials. In *Black Girl*, a similar statue in front of the Senegalese National Assembly is worth a thousand words to illustrate the filmmaker's viewpoint about his country's post-independence reality.

Sembene's treatment of graphic and visual signs, such as posters, is also meaningful throughout his films. In *Emitai*, a poster advertising the colonial army and showing the profile of the head of a white French soldier wearing a colonial helmet is very significant and satirical. A poster of Samori and Cabral in Rama's room (*Xala*) and a poster of Lumumba in the room of Diouana's boyfriend (*Black Girl*), provide immediate information concerning political orientations of the young protagonists.

In Sembene's films, as in many other African films, clothing serves to typecast characters and make social statements: "You are what you look." The contrast between the beggars' rags and the businessmen's suits is constant in *Xala*. The *boubou*, a long robe worn by many of the characters who are traditionalists, is a cultural choice rather than the true reflection of a particular economic level. In most instances, the European-style pants and shirt are less expensive than the boubou. In *Mandabi*, Dieng's boubou, rather than a protection, becomes an obstacle as he is winding through the streets of modern Dakar. It accentuates his cultural maladjustment. On the contrary, as frequently as humble people wear boubous, the new elite prefers to wear European clothes, except when they momentarily want to appear as traditionalists like the businessmen of *Xala* (when they oust the French from the Chamber of Commerce). This trend is followed primarily by men. Only two women belonging to the upper class wear European dresses; namely, Oumi in *Xala* and the wife of the corrupted businessman in *Mandabi*. Those are shallow characters whose Africanness is "masked" by the European wigs they wear. Yet, in general, whatever their social class, Sembene's women characters wear boubous which they adorn with rich jewels even in modest surroundings like those of *Mandabi* or *Taw*. This probably reflects, in addition to his aesthetic choice, Sembene's reverence for the tall majestic beauty of the Senegalese women who are better served by long dresses. It also expresses his view that the Senegalese woman has remained closer to the African tradition than men. Here again, whatever symbolic associations may be made, Sembene insists that his handling of clothing is realistic and by no means an embellishment of reality. "In Senegal, people like to dress. Perhaps it is a way to assert oneself through one's looks. It is a way to stress one's social status. Here, people have to dress well. It is important. People justify this by saying: 'I don't dress for myself, I dress for other people.' People can die of hunger but this is not seen."[23]

In Sembene's motion pictures, there are as many African masks and mosques as there are statues and churches in Italian films. Those are cultural marks which delimit a particular socioreligious sphere. Sembene acknowledges employing copies of traditional art rather than original ones. For him, the manner in which they are used is more important than their authenticity.

Obviously, the filmmaker also uses familiar objects as visual signs to arouse the pleasure of the African viewers, reinforce their attention, and facilitate their identification with the protagonists on the screen. Sembene's iconographic universe serves realistic as well as metaphorical purposes for both African and non-African audiences. Furthermore, although his films are not primarily intended for non-African viewers, they also reveal to foreigners the many ordinary or ceremonial objects of Senegalese culture which, until then, may have been unknown to them.

SOUNDTRACK

Cinema, by definition, should be first and foremost a visual medium with sound playing a subordinate role. Hence, especially in realistic films, the soundtrack should not be overwhelming and distract from reality. According to many, true cinematic sound should be neither merely an accompanying sound nor basically an explanatory sound. It should be integrated into the action of the film. A soundtrack commonly includes the reproduction of words and natural or artificial sounds as well as music. Usually, half of the film relies on images while the rest of the story is expressed through the soundtrack. For a verbal and visual balance to be achieved, long stretches of talk should be avoided because they tend to weaken images and reduce the viewer's interest. Most of Sembene's films seem to abide by these principles except in the case of *Niaye* and parts of *Emitai* and *Ceddo*—although in total, words amount to only half an hour of the two-hour running time of the last. In *Emitai* and *Ceddo*, Sembene felt obliged to reproduce the long palavers of the elders at given historical times. This may appear theatrical, fatiguing, and monotonous to the non-African viewer unfamiliar with the culture. It is less so to the modern African viewer whose aesthetics derive from the oral tradition.

In *Niaye, Borom Sarret*, and *Black Girl*, Sembene compromisingly opted for an off-screen voice. In *Niaye*, it is that of the griot which, in addition to being an expository device, is used to convey information about the plot and express his standpoint and that of the filmmaker as the story unfolds. Such device assures the continuity of the plot but somewhat hampers the visual flow of the film because of the narrator/participant's didactic, dogmatic, and pompous tone. *Niaye*, which has not been widely distributed, is unsuccessful in its soundtrack because its images become artificial, overwhelmed by the ideas that the filmmaker relentlessly imposes upon the viewers' minds. In *Borom Sarret* and *Black Girl*, Sembene handles the off-screen voice in a much more lyrical and restrained fashion. In *Borom Sarret*, it is the filmmaker's own voice inserted in his film as that of the cart driver. In spite of the director's verbal intrusion into his story, *Borom Sarret* retains the flavor of the novelistic first person. It is in *Black Girl* that Sembene renders best the off-screen voice of Diouana's inner monologue and stream of consciousness. It even facilitates the viewer's identification with the character. However, critics have observed that the use of French in the soundtrack, as in *Borom Sarret*, decreases the realism of the film, since Diouana, an uneducated maid, would certainly not have thought in French. They also argue that the post-synchronization, through Haitian singer Toto Bissainte's voice as Diouana, reinforces the artificiality of the process. An opposite standpoint might be taken, however. With Toto Bissainte's voice in French, one might very well wonder if Sembene is not universalizing her plight, linking Diouana's fate to that of the many West Indian maids working in France and who undergo similar experiences.

Sembene advocates natural sounds in motion pictures. He rejects the overuse of musical scores found in Western cinema: "Whites have music for everything in their films—music for rain, music for the wind, music for tears, music for moments of emotion—but the white man doesn't know how to make these elements speak for themselves."[24] Speaking of *Emitai*, the Senegalese director says:

For example, there were the two children who were walking along to bring water to the women. When they crossed the woods, you couldn't see their legs. But you could hear, very clearly, the dead leaves. For me, this is the cinema of silence. In the Sacred Forest, life continued because there was a fire, and the wind was blowing. I didn't try to bring in any music. When the gourd fell it was empty and it made a noise. In that instance, the silence was very profound. And I think all of this indicates a search on our part, a search for African filmmaking.[25]

The abrupt interruption of sound draws attention and often increases dramatic tension. It might be said that silence itself is a sound effect. It alters the rhythm of the film and makes the viewer focus on the visual to which it may convey a ghostly, unnatural quality. For Sembene, silence may be natural sounds or the total absence of sound (deadtrack). In both cases, it is both word and thought, a dramatic element by which the audience is led to focus on the characters' facial expressions and to feel the suspense of the situation. Above all, it stresses the verisimilitude of the events Sembene wants to portray. Still referring to *Emitai*, Sembene states:

In *Emitai*, when the women are seated, the only sound you hear is the sound of the rooster and the weeping of the children—and the wind. I did not look for music to ask the public to participate. I just wanted to prove, by gestures, that the women were tired, their legs were tired, their arms burdened. A woman in whose eyes the sun was shining; the two who were sleeping—always in silence. But the silence that I wanted to show was a silence that spoke. I could have had a voice coming from the outside, but I would have been lying.[26]

Music and sound usually stop with the scene. Overlapping sound may imply a metaphor, focus, or counterpoint. The end of *Emitai*—when the African soldiers firing shots on the villagers are heard without being seen in the darkness of the movie theater—is abrupt and shocking. Inevitably, the viewers believe the film has been broken in the projectionist's booth. When they realize that the film has ended, they comment on its unexpected, somewhat "aborted" ending and through their discussion prolong the film beyond its end—precisely what the director wishes them to do. A similarly disquieting ending is found in *Xala*. After the freeze frame of El Hadji being spat upon has disappeared from the screen, the sound of the spitting continues for a few seconds and the viewers might very well wonder whether it is at them that the beggars are now spitting.

Such disassociations of picture and sound are not found only at the end of Sembene's films. In the first sequence of *Xala*, long before the credits, a drummer is seen playing, in a medium shot, before we hear the music he plays and before we see him in a long shot among the players and griots welcoming the new African members of the Chamber of Commerce. It is to be noted here that Sembene goes visually from the part to the whole rather frequently instead of the opposite process, which is more often used in Western cinema. Sembene thus associates startling effects at the level of both image and sound. *Borom Sarret* presents another case where sound does not correspond to what is on the screen. At the beginning of this film, while the screen is still in total darkness and then during the unfolding of the credits, the muezzin's insistent and haunting call for prayer is heard long before he is actually seen.

Another sound effect employed by Sembene to startle his audience is that of distorted or amplified sound. The shrieking and nasal voices of the masks of *Emitai*, as they become animated by the gods' spirits, reflect the procedures of many African rituals in which the human voice is said to be transformed because of divine intercession. This instigates the direct merging of the spectators into the supernatural realm of traditional African religions. Then in *Emitai*, for example, the amplified sound of the soldiers' shots being fired comes as the filmmaker's supreme and distinct statement.

In film, music has a more varied effect on the viewers' responses than the reproduction of natural or artificial sounds which are used by the filmmaker to create atmosphere. Music is an emotional punctuation which stimulates imagination. It may create or stress a mood, announce events, and help to build dramatic tension. Discussing music in general, Sembene points out that "music is made to stress, to accentuate, or to intensify the action of the film. Looking at some soundtracks, one notices that music works like a signal. There is, for instance, a kind of music appropriate to mystery. With Hitchcock, it announces suspense. Music also is adapted to a particular setting or architecture."[27]

Sembene says that "often in European films the music is gratuitous."[28] For him, music is not an ornament. It has a definite function in that it provides greater impact and increased meaning. "I don't try to have a music which accompanies the picture. I try to detach it from the picture so that it holds by its own instead of calling for the complete adhesion of the viewers, who can then predict what will take place on the screen. The music of a film should stress its pictures."[29]

No music is especially conceived by Sembene to accompany credits. Many times, the credits of his films come as a superimposition on pictures after the films have already started—as happens in *Taw*, *Emitai*, *Xala*, and *Ceddo*. These credits are presented with a soundtrack which fits the story at the time. Sembene rejects the sound scores played by orchestras which are used to create the glorious exotic moods of Hollywood's films on Africa as soon as the credits appear on the screen. Sembene favors music performed by small groups of players or singers with preference for Wolof songs. In terms of instruments, except in *Black Girl, Emitai, Xala,* and *Ceddo,* films in which he occasionally uses drums, Sembene shows a definite inclination to the *xalam* (a Wolof string instrument) because its sound is not overwhelming and because its basic rhythm is well adapted to his films. Asked about such musical choice, the filmmaker explains simply: "I think the xalam is more suitable to films than the drum. Drums make too much noise."[30]

In some instances, sounds are used rhythmically and melodiously to create a musical effect without the help of a musical instrument. Concerning the greatest part of the musical score of *Ceddo*, Sembene specifies that "it is not exactly music. It is a repetition of sounds and rhythms. It is done with bottles. Why not harmonize sounds and rhythms, why should we always resort to traditional African music for our films?"[31]

The modernistic, "jazzy" rhythms of *Ceddo* place the Ceddo's fierce determination to retain their identity in Senegal's present-day context. Its varied patterns, along with the bass drum and trumpets, universalize *Ceddo* and facilitate its understanding beyond the ethnic group it describes. According to Sembene:

The form of the film is tied to its topic. But we have an audience coming from varied backgrounds and speaking different languages. So as soon as the film is no longer shown in its ethnic context, the words are no longer understood by people. Yet these people see and hear. They are sensitive to what they hear because they are still immersed in an oral culture where the spoken word predominates. What should we provide for the spectators who hear but do not understand what they hear? Well, one must try to reach them through gestures and semantics and provide them with something they will understand. This is why we changed the kind of music used in *Ceddo*. We made four different musical scores for *Ceddo* before finding the adequate one.[32]

Sembene's choice of Cameroonian musician Manu Dibango and Afro-American composer Arthur Simms to make the music of *Ceddo* has a universal symbolic value. The striking gospel song "I'll Take It Home Someday," heard when the slaves are branded with a *fleur-de-lis*, also refers to the black diaspora. In Sembene's words, "the infusion of gospel represents a breaking off. Here we dealt with the problem of slavery because we had never done it before. From that moment on, the film opens on the diaspora. . . ."[33]

Later on, in *Ceddo*, the song of the African Catholic mass interpreted by the St. Joseph de Cluny choir comments on today's Christianity in Dakar. This is brought in as a flashforward illustrating the missionary's dream as he watches the empty benches of his village church. Here again, the process is particularly striking because no fade in, fade out, or picture blurring prepares the audience for such sequence. Later, as the imam's followers attack the Ceddo at night, a frenzied musical dissonance and amplified cracking of fire underscores the chaotic confrontation in a very effective audiovisual collision.

Music identifies groups of people, geographical areas, and historical periods and evokes atmospheres. In *Borom Sarret*, Sembene suddenly switches from the sound of a Wolof guitar to music by Mozart as the cart driver reaches downtown Dakar, the former European section of town. Sembene uses recorded music. " . . . I wanted to show the European area and Africans who had adopted a European lifestyle. The only music I could relate to them was the classical music, the minuets of the 18th century, because it conforms to their mentality."[34]

Music as a humorous counterpoint in an otherwise dramatic situation is also exploited by Sembene in his satirical use of French songs and marches. In *Niaye*, the chief's son offers a clumsy rendition of "Auprès de ma Blonde" (Near My Fair Lady), a French folk song; and in *Emitai*, the African soldiers interpret "Maréchal Nous Voilà" (Marshal Here We Are), a song in which some French people expressed their support to Marshal Pétain during World War II. In both instances the effect of these songs, in a most unexpected setting, is hilarious and emphasizes Sembene's mockery of French assimilation.

The words of the Senegalese songs heard in Sembene's films are all meaningful and may intermingle reality and fiction. The director points out:

The musical theme which accompanies my protagonist Diouana derives from the plaintive ballad composed, with the accompaniment of a drum, by a friend of the actual victim after her suicide. I took care of the musical arrangement: the music was performed by a chorus and a drum. But the soloist is purposely louder than the chorus. The girl who sings is the one who created the song. The rest of the music is traditional string music.[35]

In *Black Girl*, the ballad played at the end of the film evokes the words of the poem composed by Sembene in Diouana's memory. The filmmaker observes that "the book was written in 1958. The film was shot in 1965. Thus, an evolution took place in me. The poem per se is not included in the film, but it is expressed in the song which was specially created in Serer for Diouana."[36]

The songs which are heard on the soundtrack of *Mandabi* and *Xala* were written by Sembene in collaboration with Samba Diabare Sam. Composed in Wolof, they are a part of the narrative pattern of those films. The songs denounce the social injustice revealed in the plot. In *Emitai*, the villagers' rebellion is instigated by a song. Sembene remarks that, "when the women saw that the men surrendered their rice, they started to sing a song which praised the heroism of their ancestors, who preferred death to a life of shame."[37]

Sembene's creative input in musical film scoring is particularly significant in *Ceddo*, where a true unity between musical idiom and picture is achieved. The score of *Ceddo*, a mixture of traditional African music and modern syncopations, is so finely textured that it can be listened to independently and can evoke the atmosphere of the film.[38]

Sembene, especially in his later works, uses not only sound from sources visible on the screen but also symbolic sound from sources not on the screen, whenever such sound reinforces the story and expands its dimensions beyond what is seen by the audience. In *Ceddo*, for instance, on several occasions music further carries the significance of the visual image (for example, the gospel music sequence). For Sembene, music becomes "a storytelling element capable of providing information by itself."[39]

LYRICISM AND EPIC

Particularly in early films like *Borom Sarret* and *Black Girl*, Sembene has succeeded in creating an impressionistic atmosphere full of poetic lyricism. The intimate mood of these films owes much to the use of the off-screen voice/inner voice of the principal characters, which establishes an emotional closeness with the viewers. The subjective, reflective narrative draws the viewers into the character's experience in a very effective manner. Although lyrical, these two films are not sentimental and their men/women relationship is treated in a seemingly restrained fashion which does not detract from the dialectical significance of the story.

As a rule, sex or physical violence are not the main ingredients of Sembene's films except *Xala*—where sex is treated more for its symbolic than its erotic significance—or in *Emitai* and *Ceddo*—where physical violence is shown only when it cannot be avoided. "But Sembene never gives way in the slightest to the temptation to present violence for the sake of violence. All the scenes of violence are essential, indispensable, for—and we must not forget this—*Emitai* is not so much a condemnation of colonial exploitation as a glorification of the fundamentally human act which revolt in part represents."[40] It should be noted that Sembene prefers psychological collision triggered by cultural differences to purely physical conflicts.

In many of Sembene's films, nature is not merely a setting but a world in which man feels at ease and in harmony with the land, sky, waters, and trees around him. This cosmic correlation between man and nature is found also in most African religions and philosophies. The manner in which Sembene depicts nature calls to mind the poetic symbolism present in many Soviet films, particularly those of Donskoi, who trained Sembene. In *Emitai*, for example, the rivers, sun, and sky symbolize the eternal strength of nature through the ritualistic merging of rice and waters in a timeless cycle of cosmic fecundity. On several occasions, birds disperse in a cloudless sky as the messengers of a new era (*Niaye*) or danger (*Ceddo*), while water is perceived as a symbol of purification and renewal (*Niaye, Ceddo*).

This kind of intimate and symbolic lyricism, however, is not the dominant mood of his films. While it suits events of daily life or natural phenomena, it is less well adapted to some of the exemplary moments of *Emitai* and *Ceddo*, which call for an heroic atmosphere. *Ceddo*, for instance, reaches the level of an epic because it gives such preeminence to verbal flourishes, oratorical encounters, and elevated heroic mood. One has to remember here that African epics were created to be recited in societies, such as that of Senegal, where the transmission of ideals and morals through the written word was limited in scope if not ignored. Also, the conflation of temporal setting and the fusion of historical facts (readily acknowledged by Sembene in his desire to "dramatize history") is a frequent occurrence in heroic epics throughout the world. In addition to these comparisons, a similarity can be established between the social systems existing in most areas which generated epics. *Ceddo*, like the well-known French *Le Chanson de Roland* (The Song of Roland), or the Mandingo epic *Soundjata*, emerges from a context that exalts the deeds of feudal nobility to maintain cultural and political identity in the wake of foreign expansion (in both *Ceddo* and *La Chanson de Roland*, Islam is the invader). Almost all epics, like *Ceddo*, contain courtly love and conflicts between personal ambitions and feudal or religious obligations. *Ceddo*, an African *chanson de geste*, extols and perpetuates fidelity to traditional group values and religious ideals.

In addition, comparisons can be drawn between *Ceddo* and Shadi Abdessalam's film *The Mummy* (1969, Egypt), because of similarly slow incantatory gestures and an overall epic tone common to both. The elders and the masks of *Emitai* have parallels in the chorus and masks of epic Greek tragedy. Also, *Emitai*'s plot contains analogies with the sufferings of the women and children of the defeated leaders of Troy at the hands of their conquerors depicted in Euripides's play *The Trojan Women*. Its content is, moreover, reminiscent of the conflict between the laws of the state and those of the gods found in Sophocles's *Antigone*. The concentrated plot of *Ceddo* brings to mind the law of the unities of place, action, and time commonly found in seventeenth-century French theater. In spite of such possible comparisons, *Ceddo* belongs principally to the African drama with its re-enactments of historical events, particularly battles. It is of the same lineage as the Zulu epic *Chaka*, whose pedagogical function was to enlighten audiences with the glories of a remote past. At times, the low angle shots of the Ceddo and the princess against the sky accentuate their symbolic as well as historical significance.

In mood and treatment, two strains can be detected in Sembene's films, depending on the topic he chooses to portray. When he is dealing with everyday life in a contemporary setting, he uses a naturalistic style and a pace which is quicker than that of his stately historical epics. In *Emitai* and *Ceddo*, which illustrate exceptional situations, more elaborate means are used, possibly with the aim of elevating film art to the exemplary situation and ceremonial aspect of the kind of theater whose aim is to exalt collective values.

COMEDY AND SATIRE

Although irony is not absent from epic-oriented films such as *Emitai* and *Ceddo*, it is primarily in his motion pictures about contemporary Senegal that Sembene inserts comical elements which can easily be understood by his African audiences. In *Mandabi* and *Xala* the entire film is a bittersweet comedy of manners, while in the others, such as *Niaye, Borom Sarret, Black Girl*, and *Emitai*, comical interludes relieve the tension of an otherwise tragic story.

Often in Sembene's films, laughter derives from an unexpected situation, like the appearance of the thief as the new member of the Chamber of Commerce to replace El Hadji who has just been expelled for embezzlement (*Xala*). Cuckoldry and impotence have always been choice topics for comic authors and playwrights, and Sembene makes an imprint in such tradition to the extent Jack Kroll writes about *Xala*: "This allegory of impotence in the body politic shows Sembene on his way to becoming an African Molière."[41]

The repetition of situations can also generate laughter. This happens in *Mandabi*, where Dieng is accosted twice by the same woman beggar who overcomes his anger by accusing him of propositioning her. In this case also, the end result being different from that intended bears humorous connotations which underline Dieng's vulnerability at being tricked by everybody.

Farcical gestures, amplified movements, and disguise have been universally used in comedy, and Sembene exploits such devices in his works. According to Pierre Haffner, the satirical Koteba theater from Mali is, for a large part, based on comical gestures, whose significance can reach large audiences who might speak different languages.[42] Considering the culturally restrictive scope within which verbal wit functions, it can be assumed that Sembene responds to similar concerns in using the immediacy and universality of comic gestures.

Everyone familiar with Sembene's films remembers the farcical scene of *Xala* where El Hadji, applying his marabout's prescription against impotence, crawls half naked to his new wife. El Hadji's grotesque appearance as he crawls like an animal, followed by an abortive enticement to sexual activity, inevitably triggers loud bursts of laugh on the part of any audience. Furthermore, a dance scene in which the tiny president of the Chamber of Commerce disappears in the arms and bosom of El Hadji's portly second wife is hilarious. So is a scene in which El Hadji's Mercedes, a product of German engineering genius, has to be pushed by the Senegalese soldiers who had come to seize it because none of them is able to drive it.

Sembene's attack on the new elite is expressed through his acerbic portrayals of Europeanized Senegalese. In *Taw*, it is the snobbishness of the transitional Senegalese woman of comfortable means which is at stake. On their way home from a shopping trip, two elegant Dakar women in rich and irridescent boubous hire the services of Taw's younger brother to carry their baskets. Offended by the natural smells of the African market place, one of them says disdainfully to the other: "I hate shopping because I go home smelling like a fish." In *Mandabi*, the filmmaker gives a satirical description of the self-importance of civil servants when one of the clerks resents interrupting his reading of a magazine to help Dieng. Others discuss their fraudulent banking operations while people are waiting in line. In *Black Girl*, two representatives discuss their private materialist ambitions. In *Xala*, one of El Hadji's guests, who is asked whether he spent his vacation in Spain or Switzerland, explains that he does not go to Spain anymore because there are too many blacks there. In this same film, a Senegalese businessman asks another how to say "weekend" in English, unaware of the fact that he is using this very English term in his question asked in French. The artificial distance created between people and their natural surroundings is emphasized in *Xala* through the repeated humorous use El Hadji's secretary makes of sprays to kill both insects in her office and odors emerging from a sewage hole where women in the neighborhood come periodically to pour their waste water.

Besides comical situations which result from repetition of excessive gestures and habits, Sembene also uses the clashes of words ill fitted to a given character or setting. Some of those verbal ironies and stereotypical statements, however, may be less readily understood by non-Senegalese viewers who are unaware of the author's intended cultural connotations. The humor of certain proverbs in *Ceddo* loses much of its flavor when translated into a Western language. The humor is lost also for modern African viewers outside of the Wolof ethnic group and present-day Wolof unaccustomed to the flowery language of their ancestors used in the film. Also, people unfamiliar with the role of *hommes-femmes* (men with women's mannerisms) in Senegalese festivities may not fully appreciate the "sh-i-it" one of them says with a black American accent during El Hadji's wedding ceremony. Yet, they will not miss Sembene's derision as that same character asserts, sighing, that there are no longer "true men" around. Furthermore, the grim humor of the "welcome" sign at the entrance of the place where beggars are brought after being evicted from the city by the police is understood by all.

On other occasions, Sembene's satire expresses itself through unexpected crude language as that of the sophisticated Oumi who, losing her polish, angrily observes to her husband: "Your third wife is just like the rest of us. Her split is not horizontal but vertical."

Sembene's use of verbal irony reaches its peak, as seen before, in a conversation between the two African soldiers who criticize French institutions in *Emitai*. Their discussion centers on Pétain, a seven-star marshal being replaced by De Gaulle, a lower-ranked brigadier general. Sembene's sarcasm is also particularly mordant in his actors' rendering of the speeches delivered by these officials he chooses to mock. In *Emitai*, the words of the French commander describing Pétain as the "father of both Africans and French" underscores the implied treatment which the soldiers are made to face. In *Xala*, the voice of the president of the Chamber of Commerce has the same intonation as Senghor's and his claim for independence is in sharp contrast with Senegal's economic and cultural dependency suggested in the film. Hence, Sembene's parodying approach through the president's words: "Never before has an African occupied the presidency of our Chamber. We must control our industry, our commerce, our culture, take in hand our destiny. This is an historic day. It is a victory for our people. Sons of the people are leading the people in the people's behalf. We chose socialism, the only true socialism, the African socialism. Socialism on man's level. Our independence is complete."

Even in Sembene's lyrical and tragic stories, one finds comical attitudes like that of the cartman of *Borom Sarret*, who mechanically implores all possible gods and saints to protect him in the face of danger and forthcoming difficulty. A mordant cameo of French petty bourgeois mentality is particularly effective in *Black Girl*.

For Sembene, a comedy has a definite function. Commenting on the caricatural style of *Xala*, he points out: "Yes, it makes people laugh but it also makes them think. For us, laughter is a social phenomenon: people like to talk and laugh. At the movies, they remember better what has made them laugh than what has made them cry. And there is a lot of discussion taking place as people leave the movie theater."[43]

Sembene's comic devices also trigger laughter as a group reaction against an individual character or group of people who are not adapted to the majority's sociocultural norms or who transgress them. The filmmaker's direct or indirect satires denounce false values and postures. Since they take place in a contemporary setting, they facilitate the Senegalese audiences' identification and tend to generate laughter which is socially purifying. Many times, comedy is expected to provide a group with means of fighting evil. People laugh at their faults and bad habits and this may encourage their correction. This happens in the case of Sembene's films and the plays of the Koteba theater. Both aim to entertain and educate their spectators.[44] As suggested before, Sembene's caustic tone may also be compared to the mordant irony of the African griot, whose social role lets him speak out and rebuke superiors for misdeeds.

Some of the topics which Sembene has elected to treat in comic mode are timeless and universal. Political corruption has been a dramatic subject since at least the time of Aristophanes, and the foibles of the new bourgeoisie were exploited for their comic value by Molière. Such topics—vanity, pedantry, venality, the abuse of power—transcend the environment of Senegal. Nevertheless, Sembene's sarcasm is directed especially at their manifestation in a Senegalese society, something of which the censors in Dakar are fully aware. He particularly focuses on the pretenses, the corruption, and the self-importance of this new elite of Senegalese society. When dignitaries are ridiculed, it is their authority and the institutions they represent which are mocked. This is precisely what Sembene does in films like *Ceddo* through the dwarflike appearance of the totalitarian imam, the opportunistic courtier who tells his peers: "Let's work at safeguarding a few advantages," and the disconcerting missionary who reads his breviary and makes the sign of the cross while slaves march by him, herded in for trade.

Sembene's satire is designed as sharp social criticism with subversive overtones since what is ridiculed is, beyond the boundaries of time, linked to the norms and customs of the Senegalese establishment. The Senegalese censors' amputations applied to his latest films attest to the impact of his sly comic insight. Even when it is the goggling buffoonery of Dieng (*Mandabi*) which is at stake, it is implied that he is the victim of forces beyond his control: those in the hands of the new Senegalese elite.

Thus, the irony found in many of Sembene's films also expresses the filmmaker's ironic world views and inner skepticism. His stylistic and thematic clashes reflect his disenchanted idealism, his disappointment with what post-independent Senegal is in relation to what he had expected it to be. For him, indeed, life is a series of ambiguities, paradoxes, and incoherences best denounced with the hope of some remedy through biting sarcasm.

RESOURCES AND METHODS OF WORK

In spite of his renown as a writer and a filmmaker, Sembene works in the same socioeconomic context as other African directors. His personal means, such as royalties from books, films, and lecture fees, are indisputably higher than those of the average African filmmaker. Yet he also has to resort to outside financial sources to subsidize his films, namely the French and/or Senegalese government.

Sembene's films necessarily have low budgets, especially when compared to Western films: $20,000 for *Borom Sarret* and less than $50,000 for *Black Girl*. His most recent films have been financially more ambitious. *Ceddo*, for example, had a budget of $500,000. His next production, *Samori*, is expected to cost about $4,000,000, the highest budget ever allocated to an African film. Sembene explains: "A film about African history requires a lot of financial means, research, and reconstitution. I can make but so many, although I try to intersperse them in my production."[45]

Generally, Sembene has to adapt his craft to limited means. This is facilitated by his type of movie making and his naturalistic rendering of life, which do not require grandiose effects and intricate camera work. His crews are usually small in number—which is probably less disturbing for non-professional actors and for people living in the places where the film is shot. *Borom Sarret* was made with a single camera and a three-man crew: Sembene as scenarist and director, Christian Lacoste as cameraman, and Ibrahima Barro as assistant. Sembene was able to keep the cost of this film to a minimum because he benefited from the free participation of actors and used lab post-synchronization, thus avoiding the expenses necessitated by on-the-spot recording equipment.

Sembene's work is also greatly eased by a number of reliable people to whom he can turn whenever he undertakes a new film project: Christian Lacoste worked as cameraman in both *Borom Sarret* and *Black Girl*; Georges Caristan shot *Niaye, Taw, Emitai, Xala,* and *Ceddo*; while Paulin Soumanou Vieyra was the production manager of films including *Taw, Emitai,* and *Xala.* In *Mandabi,* Sembene was helped by a very able Senegalese filmmaker, Ababacar Samb, who worked with him as assistant director.

Undoubtedly, the material constraints Sembene has to face force him to use his ingenuity and have an impact on his aesthetic choices. A crew with little money may dodge what it cannot represent and may suggest what it does not show. In contrast, crews with important budgets multiply visible detail in their representation of fictional reality. As French critic Jean Patrick Lebel observes, "some talented filmmakers have proven that a scarcity of means was not necessarily opposed to the creation of a rich cinematographic language."[46] Sembene might be included among those. He also agrees that limited means do not necessarily hamper the quality of films and that such means may even stimulate creativity.

I think that a lack of means forces us to certain savings and to the use of a lot of imagination. As far as I am concerned, this situation helps me. Each time I make a film, I have to figure things out and see whether or not I am able to decrease expenses. I have to think about shortcuts, aims, and the work implied to achieve all this. Don't be mistaken, in film, the abundance of means may also be harmful.[47]

In the case of *Emitai,* Sembene had to rewrite its scenario three times. He has been working for several years on his next project, about Samori, a nineteenth-century West African hero. Yet on the average, the filmmaker estimates it takes him about a year to complete a film. This includes writing the scenario, planning, shooting, and editing.

Although the scripts for his films are carefully written, Sembene allows for a certain flexibility to adapt to the possible changes required by location shooting and the use of nonprofessional actors. Members of the crew can suggest what should be changed. He stresses:

When I write the script in my study, I can imagine whatever I want. I can foresee where to put the camera. I can do everything. It is the realm of the imagination. There, nothing is forbidden to me. . . . To work on a set with a crew is another matter. When people use a studio, the set is built by an architect according to the scenario. In a studio, everything is determined, such as where the camera should be. The light is adjusted to the setting. Everything is ready and thus only a few changes are possible. In my case, I may shoot in a house which some people lend me or else I may shoot outdoors. Then, there may be a difference between what I foresaw, what the actor envisioned, and reality. When we work in the field, we have to become soldiers maneuvering on alien ground because what we want to master is not yet ours. From then on, we have to bring some changes.[48]

When Sembene makes a film, he works intensely and may occasionally have what could be termed "temperamental outbursts." According to Georges Caristan, Sembene's favorite cameraman, "some people say that he is impossible to work with, but I do not agree with them. He knows how to impose himself. He 'lives' his films, and one has to understand this and share his concerns. When problems occur while shooting a film, we discuss them; he listens to us and we always find a solution."[49]

Even if, at times, his crew influences his decision making Sembene feels that he is completely responsible for his films.

Whether the filmmaker is the immediate or the ultimate creator of a work which requires the collaboration of many and depends on a given socioeconomic context has been debated for many years. In film, scriptwriters and editors work together with directors. However, the directors are the ones signing the film. Judicially, it is to them that the film is attributed. My case is different from most other directors. I write my script, shoot and edit my films. Although, for me, everybody involved in the making of a film is important, I control the entire film process and I feel completely responsible for it.[50]

This feeling of total responsibility explains precisely why, in his methods of work, Sembene is as demanding of others as he is of himself.

SYNTHESIS

For Sembene, film is notoriously an art but also a medium of recording reality through which immediate and/or symbolic messages can be conveyed. Thus, his main concern is to tell an interesting, unified, and plausible story, with one major theme and no confusing subplots, which will be readily understood by all Senegalese viewers. This is why his films are characterized by an overall clarity of narration adapted to African audiences as a comprehensible, identifiable whole. Sembene advocates the use of clarity in translating the immediacy and concreteness of ordinary situations in films dealing principally with everyday Senegalese life. For him, although he may use vignettes common to the satirical picaresque narrative (*Mandabi*), a linear progression is essential. According to Sembene, "in Africa, spectators have a predilection for films that tell stories."[51]

The story of the film is so important for Sembene that he would even like to omit the credits which, according to him, detract from the story. He prefers the immediate propulsion of the viewer into the plot. "My dream would be to make a film without credits, but laws are such that I have to use them. Sometimes, I insert the credits long after the film has started so as not to interfere with the action."[52]

Except for cases such as the spitting at the end of *Xala*, Western observers have said that Sembene's films are more subversive in content than in style and that he is more an iconoclast at the level of ideas than that of innovative images. Sembene recognizes that his use of contrasting editing partly results from the definite admiration in which he holds Eisenstein.[53] With the exception of Donskoi, he denies having been influenced by any other filmmaker in particular.

When I see some of the films by Louis Malle, François Truffaut, and Jean-Luc Godard, I analyze the way their films are made, their technical aspect, their sensitivity, and the actors' portrayal. I am pleased with what I see but I would not say that they influence me. Their society is different from mine and the concern for their society is different from the one I have for mine. I am learning a lot from everybody, including the African filmmakers. I go to see the African filmmakers. I go to see many African films in order not to duplicate them. I will not give their names. We are not many African filmmakers and, as a rule, we do not publicly criticize each other in order not to create schisms.[54]

Although some critics have stressed a lack of stylistic novelty, Sembene's films should be appreciated for more than a mere social or anthropological value. An aesthetic continuity is to be noted in his works: use of image contrast, meaningful juxtaposition of complementary sequences, innovative handling of social and sacred space, utilization of a film language suited to storytelling, and so on. Sembene does not use form for form's sake or beautiful visuals for the sake of beautiful visuals. Instead, he fundamentally applies them to the transmission of ideas, which he succeeds in doing in the most effective manner.

This preeminence of thought and his use of an aesthetics related to African culture may be the true originality of Sembene's approach to filmmaking. He rejects studio slickness as well and his films are not polished according to the norms of standard Western commercial cinema. Thus, it is dangerous to judge Sembene's works solely by methods of criticism which would exclude any consideration of African culture. If Sembene's style appears conventional to a Western film critic, it is also because the latter uses his own frame of reference without considering the inherently functional aspect of African "art." Sembene is neither Renoir, Glauber Rochas, John Ford, nor Satyajit Ray. His films derive from and are made to meet the needs of a different reality. Therefore, to evaluate effectively Sembene's works, it is indispensable to place them in their own sociocultural setting whose value system is different from that of the Western world. One has to consider Sembene's ethics and aesthetics and see how they are related to Senegal's culture. It is only in this case that any evaluation of Sembene's cinema can be attempted. Such will be done, in the next pages, through an interpretive study of Sembene's most significant motion pictures, which illustrate the main stages of his cinematographic itinerary.

NOTES

1. Guy Hennebelle, "Socially Committed or Exotic Films From French-Speaking Africa," *Young Cinema and Theatre*, n. 3 (1970), p. 27.
2. From an interview with Ousmane Sembene conducted by Harold Weaver and the author in Atlanta, 11 November 1979.
3. Louis Marcorelles, "Ousmane Sembene Romancier, Cinéaste, Poète," *Les Lettres Françaises*, n. 1177 (12 April 1967), p. 24.
4. From an interview with Ousmane Sembene conducted by the author in Senegal in 1978.
5. From a lecture delivered by Ousmane Sembene in Atlanta, 11 November 1979.
6. Noureddine Ghali, "Ousmane Sembene," *Cinéma 76*, n. 208 (1976), p. 86.
7. Ibid.
8. From an interview with M. Assane Seck conducted by the author in Senegal during the summer of 1978.
9. Rudolf Arnheim, *Film as Art* (Berkeley and Los Angeles: University of California Press, 1957), p. 87.
10. Sembene to author, Senegal, 1978.
11. From "Seven Days Interview: Sembene," *Seven Days* (10 March 1978), p. 26.
12. Guy Flatley, "Senegal Is Senegal, Not Harlem," *New York Times* (2 November 1969), p. D17.
13. Ibid.
14. Sembene to author, Senegal, 1978.
15. Ibid.
16. Ibid.
17. Ibid.
18. Françoise Pfaff, "Entretien avec Ousmane Sembene: A Propos de Ceddo," *Positif*, n. 235 (1980), p. 56. Author's translation.
19. Sembene to author, Senegal, 1978.
20. Ibid.
21. Ibid.
22. Alain Masson, "Mascarade à Dakar," *Positif*, n. 182 (1976), p. 54.
23. Sembene to author, Senegal, 1978.
24. Harold Weaver, "Interview with Ousmane Sembene," *Issue*, vol. 2, n. 4 (1972), p. 60.
25. Ibid.
26. Ibid.
27. Sembene to author, Senegal, 1978.
28. Harold Weaver, "Interview with Ousmane Sembene," p. 60.

29. Sembene to author, Senegal, 1978.
30. Ibid.
31. Ousmane Sembene, "Entretien avec Sembene Ousmane," *Les 2 Ecrans*, n. 12 (1979), p. 21. Author's translation.
32. From a lecture delivered by Ousmane Sembene at Howard University, Washington, D.C., 19 February 1978.
33. Françoise Pfaff, "Entretien avec Ousmane Sembene: A Propos de Ceddo," p. 57.
34. Harold Weaver, "Interview with Ousmane Sembene," p. 60.
35. Louis Marcorelles, "Ousmane Sembene, Romancier, Cinéaste, Poète," p. 24. Author's translation.
36. From an interview with Sembene conducted by the author in Washington, D.C., 19 February 1978.
37. Sembene's lecture, Atlanta, 11 November 1979.
38. The musical score of *Ceddo* is available on both record (Fiesta 362 002 stereo) and cassette (FIC 362 002). It is distributed by SOFRASON, a member of the International Pilgrims Group.
39. Joseph M. Boggs, *The Art of Watching Films* (Menlo Park, Calif.: Benjamin/Cummings Publishing Co., 1978), p. 123.
40. Moktar Diack, "Emitai or Africa Arisen," *Young Cinema and Theatre*, n. 4 (1972), p. 29.
41. Jack Kroll, "The World on Film," *Newsweek* (13 October 1975), p. 104.
42. Pierre Haffner, *Essai sur les Fondements du Cinéma Africain* (Abidjan-Dakar: Les Nouvelles Editions Africaines, 1978), p. 63.
43. Jean and Ginette Delmas, "Ousmane Sembene: Un Film est un Débat," *Jeune Cinema*, n. 99 (December 76–January 77), p. 14. Author's translation.
44. Pierre Haffner, *Essai sur les Fondements du Cinéma Africain*, p. 63.
45. Sembene to author, Senegal, 1978.
46. Jean Patrick Lebel, *Cinéma et Idéologie* (Paris: Editions Sociales, 1971), p. 173. Author's translation.
47. Sembene to author, Senegal, 1978.
48. Ibid.
49. Françoise Pfaff, "Ousmane Sembene: His Films, His Art," *Black Art*, vol. 3, n. 3 (1979), p. 33.
50. Sembene to author, Washington, D.C., 1978.
51. Sembene to author, Senegal, 1978.
52. Ibid.
53. From a conference held by Ousmane Sembene in Moscow, 21 July 1977.
54. Sembene to author, Senegal, 1978.

PART 2

Having begun as a baby-sitter in Senegal, Diouana becomes a secluded live-in maid and cook in France. Thérèse M'Bissine Diop in *Black Girl*. (Courtesy New Yorker Films.)

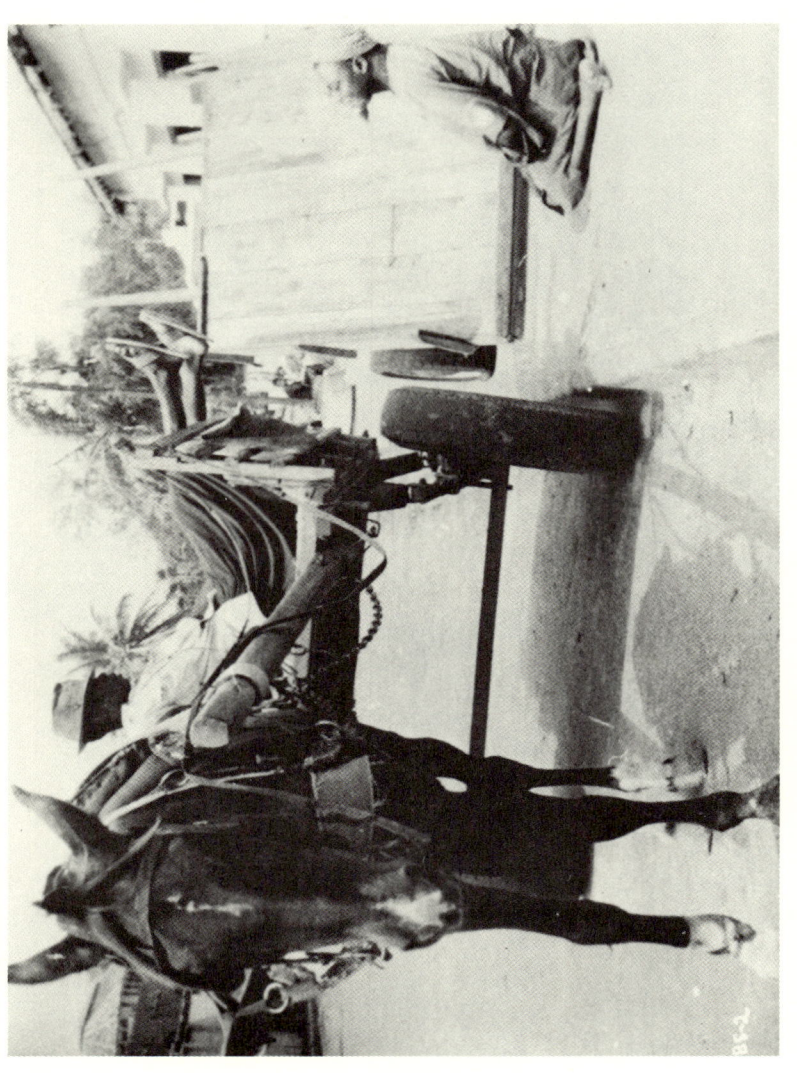

Resting in his cart, Borom Sarret is approached by a one-eyed, disfigured, and crippled beggar for whom he shows nothing but contempt. Abdoulaye Ly in *Borom Sarret*. (Courtesy New Yorker Films.)

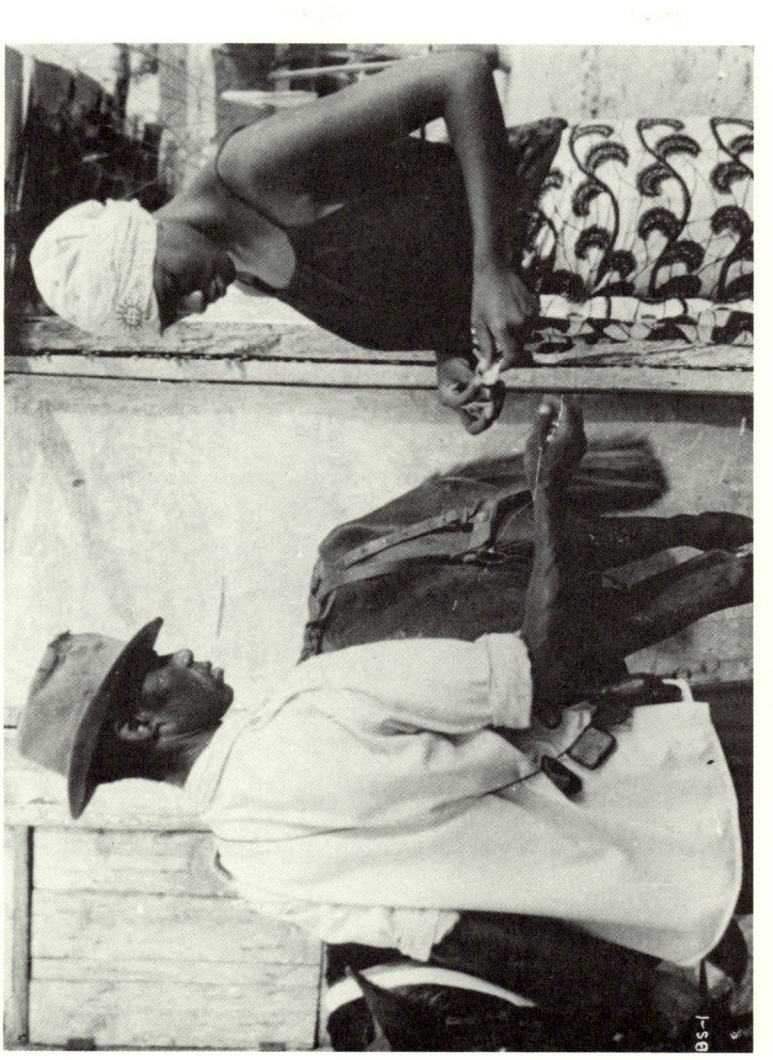

As the cartman is leaving his house, his wife gives him kola nuts before wishing him farewell. Abdoulaye Ly in *Borom Sarret*. (Courtesy New Yorker Films.)

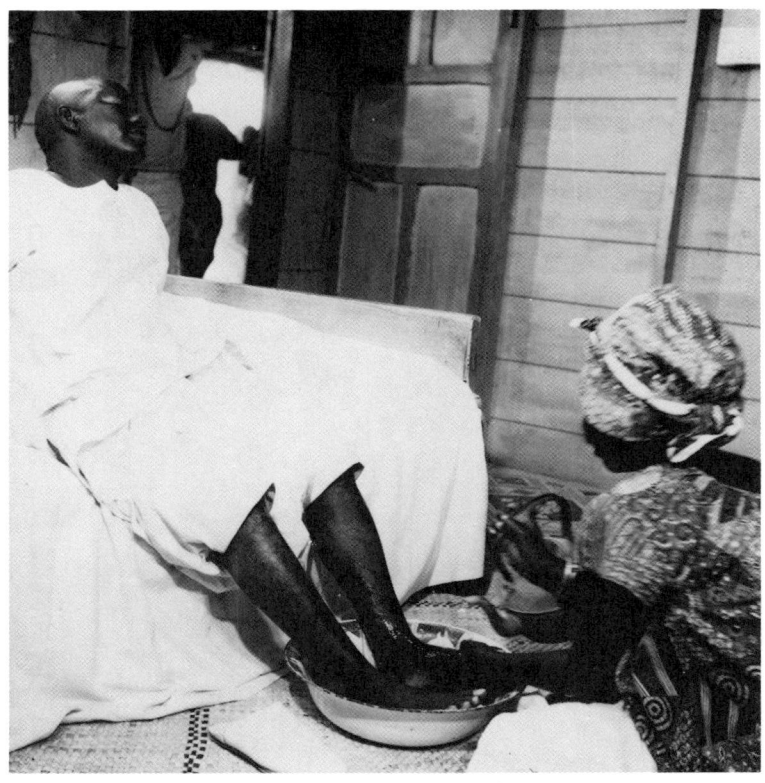

All-powerful at home, rushing his wives to prayer and domestic tasks, Ibrahima Dieng at the outset does not arouse the viewer's sympathy. Mamadou Gueye in *Mandabi*. (Courtesy Ousmane Sembene.)

Having been brutally forced into military service, recruits are taught about their new chief, Marshal Pétain, in *Emitai*. (Courtesy New Yorker Films.)

By hiding their rice, the village women become the catalyst of resistance to French colonialism in *Emitai*. (Courtesy New Yorker Films.)

Ceremonial rites accompanying the village chief's burial in *Emitai*. (Courtesy New Yorker Films.)

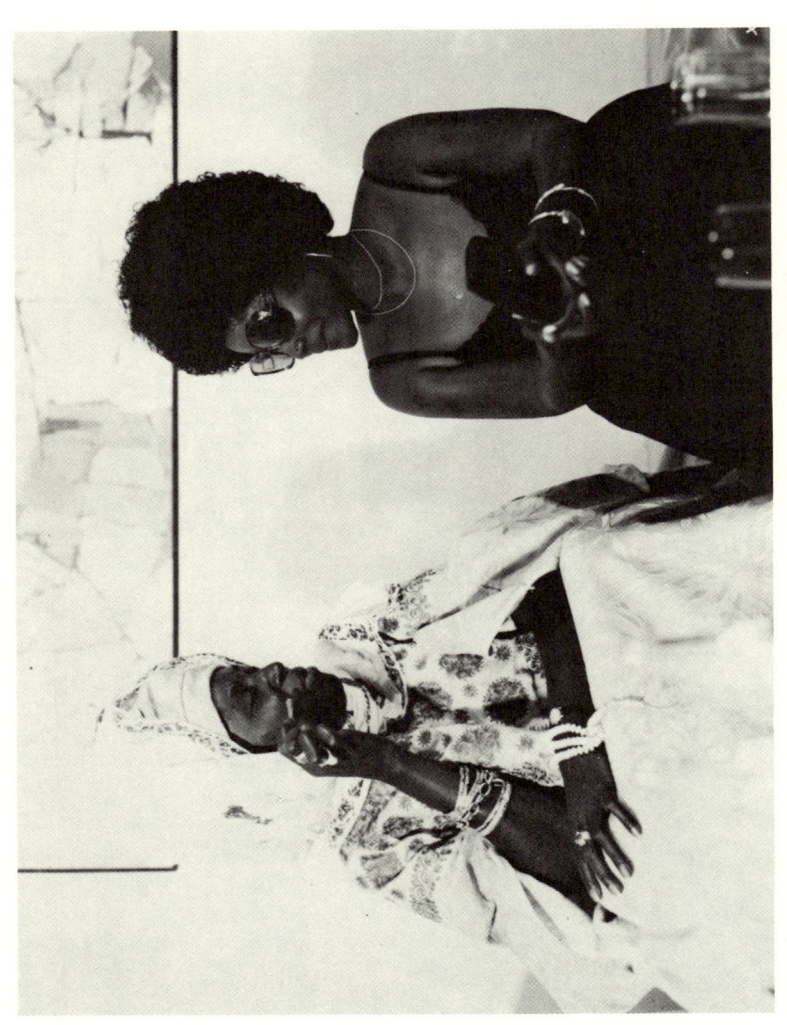

El Hadji's first two wives, Awa and Oumi, in a scene from his third wedding. Seun Samb and Younousse Seye in *Xala*. (Courtesy New Yorker Films.)

Thierno Leye as El Hadji endures the beggars' ritual trial in the hope of regaining his virility, in the final sequence of *Xala*. (Courtesy New Yorker Films.)

Ousmane Sembene directing one of the wedding party sequences of *Xala*. (Courtesy New Yorker Films.)

A scene of the slave trade in *Ceddo*. (Courtesy Ousmane Sembene.)

Rehearsing for the last sequence of *Ceddo*. Tabara N'Diaye as the princess and Goure as the imam. (Courtesy Ousmane Sembene.)

Prince Biram (*left*) is chosen over Saxewar (*right*) to deliver the princess. Mamadou Diagne and Nar Modou Sene in *Ceddo*. (Courtesy New Yorker Films.)

One important event in *Ceddo* is the abduction of the king's daughter by a Ceddo. Ismaila Diagne and Tabara N'Diaye in *Ceddo*. (Courtesy New Yorker Films.)

4
BOROM SARRET (1963): ONE DAY IN THE LIFE OF A DAKAR CARTMAN

Borom Sarret, one of Sembene's earliest films, already reveals his potential as a filmmaker and indicates the direction of his future work. Although it is made in French, it is thoroughly African in characterization and story. *Borom sarret* is a familiar Wolof expression and means literally "owner of a cart." The boroms sarrets are a familiar site in the outskirts of Dakar where they undiscriminatingly pick up customers or merchandise or both.

Sembene's twenty-minute film, shot in black and white, paints a series of vignettes of African urban life as reflected in the cartman's frustrating and ultimately tragic quest to provide for the daily survival of his family. Among the themes evoked by Sembene in this film, and which become increasingly familiar as his work develops, are those of cultural alienation, social and economic exploitation, and the tragedy of misplaced expectation. In 1963, Sembene introduced for the first time to the screen the plight of the Senegalese urban masses whose ill-prepared confrontation with modernity results in failure. As he passes from the outskirts of the city to the center of town, the cartman crosses the borderline between two worlds whose distinct characteristics are underlined by a radical change in the film soundtrack from a Wolof guitar to an orchestra playing Mozart. Then the cartman is penalized as he goes from the land of the poor to the land of the rich, and this consideration alone is indeed thought provoking.

From the very beginning of this film, Sembene uses contrasting editing to set up the religious and socioeconomic foundations of his story. *Borom Sarret* begins on the edges of Dakar from which the Great Mosque can be seen, standing upright as the unmistakably strong and prosperous symbol of Muslim faith in Senegal (90 percent of its population is Muslim). Its towering stature is duly accentuated in a low angle shot. Sembene's next picture is that of a neighborhood mosque which has none of the glamour and the imposing majesty of the previous one. From its tower, the voice of the muezzin calling for the morning prayer is heard. It is to be noted that the imam's prayer, praising Allah's greatness, starts while the first credits unfold on a dark background and before the Great Mosque actually appears on the screen. Thus, the viewer is immediately introduced in a very effective manner to the tantalizing tone and rhythm of such Islamic incantations.

A subsequent shot shows a man who, in his yard at home, kneels within a small circular area traditionally reserved for prayer and marked with white stones. Through the imam's voice, the mosques, the modest prayer circle, and the man's gestures, the filmmaker establishes aural and visual patterns defining the framework from which the plot is to develop. Then the remaining credits of the film are superimposed on a shot of an asphalt thoroughfare, vertically splitting the frame in a most striking fashion. This section of road, busy with a quick and steady flow of cars and motorbikes, is in contrast with images showing the slow motion of the cartman kneeling down within a restricted area of encircled ground. Thus, right at the beginning of the film, the motion of motor-powered vehicles representing modernity clashes with the immobility of traditional Islamic rituals, structures, and spaces symbolized through the mosques and the prayer circle.

After defining the cart driver's social spaces, Sembene focuses on his home and family. He acquaints the viewer with the modest wooden dwelling in its fenced compound and then focuses his attention on the habits of a small African family unit. In the foreground of the frame, the man, slender and dressed in shabby European pants and shirt, prays, imploring Allah's mercy and protection for himself and his family after which he puts on his amulets which reveals the syncretism of his beliefs encompassing Islam and traditional African religions. In the background of that same frame, wearing a printed *pagne* (a long African wraparound skirt) and a Western top, his wife starts her early morning duties by pounding millet in a precise and skillfully regular rhythm. In the composition of this courtyard frame, Sembene is faithful, cinematically, to the sociocultural context he is illustrating, in which the man has a superior status to the woman.

About to start his daily labor, the cart driver unties his horse. As he is leaving, his wife gives him kola nuts before wishing him farewell. She says: "Here, may God be with you and remember, we have no lunch." This scene describing the cartman's departure is short and simple. Yet it includes very precious details as to the conjugal relationship and the economic situation of the cart driver and his wife, Fathma. As is often the custom in Africa between the couple, there is no visible sign of affection which might be observed by an unexpected visitor. The man's departure is a daily observance attended by his wife. Sembene also informs us that money is scarce. If Fathma provides kola nuts for the cart driver's lunch, it means that limited food is available. Kola nuts are readily accepted by him since they contain caffein and have stimulating effects. Fathma is phlegmatic, presumably considering the sad state of affairs of her household as Allah's will. She trusts that He will provide her household with a fruitful day. She is presented as submissive but proud. Abiding in the African tradition, she respects her husband. The fact that no food is available shows that the cartman has been unable to perform his function as the family's bread winner. Yet she addresses no word of anger or contempt to him. Her attitudes reflect resignation and kindness.

As the film proceeds, Sembene provides a description of urban population through the cartman's customers or the people he encounters. The manner in which he reacts to them also provides insights about his personality. After leaving his home, the cartman rides on a dirt road winding through modest dwellings. From a high angle shot, one sees that among the cartman's habitual morning passengers, who benefit from his generosity and take advantage of his daily route from home to work, is a barefoot, elderly woman dressed in the traditional Senegalese blouse and pagne carrying a large basket. Her face has strongly marked features and reflects the kind of calm determination which comes from a day-to-day struggle for survival. She is one of the lower-class women who daily go to the market place to sell fruits, spices, and homemade fried pastries to supplement the family income. The cartman stops to offer her a ride. She slowly climbs onto the cart. Moved by her courage and tenacity, he thinks (through an offscreen voice device which depicts his reactions throughout the film): "I wonder when she'll pay me. Things are not good with her either."

The cartman's sense of commiseration relfects the respect and solicitude which is due to elders in the traditional African society. Although she does not pay him regularly, he stops to take her to the market place. Through his relationship with the elderly merchant woman is indicated the cartman's spontaneous feeling of solidarity for people who, like him, go untiringly to work every day with the hope of some small deals which will allow them to acquire basic foodstuffs and clothing. This unsophisticated observation associates him with the difficulties encountered by the old woman. Yet he views them with fatalism. Most of the cartman's other passengers also share his misery. One of them is an unemployed young man who uses his services in a daily attempt to find work. Thus, one understands why the cartman silently ponders: "Here is that no-good Mamadou. I have to take him every day. I won't stop. If I were him, I'd stay home. For six months, he has been out of work but he persists in getting up every morning." Although the cart does not stop, Mamadou jumps in the rear. Reaching the market place, the cartman stops to let his passengers off, none of whom is paying him. As Mamadou shakes his hand, the cartman observes: "I knew it, a good handshake and that's all. How am I going to feed my horse and my family?" Again, the cartman expresses resignation: "We just have to wait for God's mercy."

The cartman is now commissioned by his first paying customer to carry steel barrels and bricks. Next, Borom Sarret is stopped by a man dressed in European clothes who asks him to drive his wife to a nearby hospital. The young woman is wearing a striped boubou and sandals. As she is pregnant and about to give birth, her face expresses pain. She sits on the cart seat between the driver and her husband. To ease her discomfort accentuated by the jolting cart on a bumpy road, she rests her head on the driver's shoulder. The cartman is somewhat annoyed by the liberty she is taking, ignoring the fact that in her situation a woman might reach for any shoulder, including that of a stranger. This episode dealing with the pregnant woman provides the viewer with comic relief on hearing the cartman's soliloquy about "modern women": "And she still has her head on my shoulder. Can't she put it some place else like on her husband's shoulder? Modern women! I will never understand them!"

Here, one is led to learn that Sembene's main protagonist is attached to certain values pertaining to the traditional status and endurance of the African woman. His conservatism makes him view his customer's gesture as a moment of indecent weakness during which she lets herself indulge in familiarity with a stranger in her husband's presence. He deplores her lack of strength and self-control, qualities of the idealized traditional African woman (who, it seems, under no circumstances would let her head rest on a stranger's shoulder). He mentally criticizes what he interprets as a sign of modern times allotting to the African woman a new freedom which she is prone to misuse. Yet, when arriving at the hospital, the cartman jumps from his seat to help the husband support his wife. He does so with apparent concern and courtesy because she symbolizes the fecundity traditionally revered in African culture.

After this ride, for which he is also paid, the cartman decides to take a rest before seeking other customers. In the following scene, Sembene offers an acute comment about the relationship between the victims of a common deprivation, while simultaneously beginning to reveal some of the negative features of his protagonist. Although he has just earned some money, the cart driver shows no scruple in disregarding a beggar's request for help. The cartman is solicited in the name of Allah by a one-eyed, disfigured, and crippled beggar for whom he shows nothing but contempt. The unsparing camera becomes the cartman's eye who perceives from the high angle of his cart the beggar crawling on the ground. His two feet serve as a striking frame to the shot of the legless beggar whose level of existence is literally as well as figuratively below that of the cartman. Indifferent to the beggar's plight, the cart driver's thoughts, in contrast to his alleged religious devotion which should engender compassion, are expressed as follows: "What is the use of answering. There are so many beggars, they are like flies."

At this point, one might be tempted to justify the cartman's insensitivity by the fact that he probably wishes to save all of his pay to provide for the needs of his family. Sembene immediately proves one wrong as in the next sequence, the cartman generously awards a griot (here a praise singer) all of his money. Actually, while he is dozing on his cart, the protagonist is approached by a griot, well fed and dressed in a flamboyant boubou, who starts singing the past glories of the cartman's family. Soon, a crowd begins to gather around the griot and the cartman. Pleased at the reminiscence of his noble extraction, flattered and momentarily reinvigorated by the griot's escapist narration, the cartman forgets the worries of his present life and pays for these praises with all of the money laboriously earned that morning. In commenting later about this film, Sembene explains that, "whatever the cartman's poverty may be, when the griot came to sing his praises he felt reinstated among mankind because he found himself within his own culture again. There is a dichotomy between what he is, what he represents, what he thinks, his culture, and the weakening he undergoes in confronting urbanism and a new, emerging society."[1]

The cartman's next customer is a man who asks him to carry his dead child to the cemetary. The father does not have the necessary identity papers to bury his child. The father's ignorance of local laws, and especially the absence of family and friends in this burial, suggest that he may be a migrant worker who recently came to town, thus sharing the social alienation and precarious living conditions of Dakar's growing sub-proletariat. Borom Sarret leaves the man at the cemetary gate and departs without charging any fare.

The cartman's last client, waving bills and assuring him that he has "pull," asks him to drive downtown where carts are forbidden because they obstruct traffic. Although well aware of such law, and probably in the hope of compensating for an otherwise sterile day, the cartman accepts the ride, calling for the protection of a synchretism of supernatural powers: "Saints and marabouts assist me. I'll risk it. . . . May all the saints protect me. May all the marabouts protect me. May everybody protect me." Yet the faithful trust of the cartman is not rewarded as he is arrested by a policeman who could hardly be avoided in this section of town. The cart is confiscated by the policeman, who treats him rudely by disdainfully stepping on the cartman's war medal which, as he is showing his identification papers, has slipped out of his wallet. Again, this ride will leave him penniless, since the well-dressed and seemingly well-off customer takes advantage of his dealings with the policeman to hail a taxi and disappear without paying his fare.

On his way home, crushed and overwhelmed by the height of modern buildings, forlorn in the busy streets and blinking traffic lights, the cartman, walking alongside his horse, ponders over his sterile day. "Not only did that good-for-nothing run off without paying but now I have lost my cart. How can I pay a fine? What will become of me now? That guy said he had pull and robbed me!"

After attributing his misfortune to his last customer, the cartman establishes a link between him and the new Senegalese elite in power who promised to restore social equity and progress in reaction to the injustices of the past colonial rulers. "Who can you trust? It is the same all over. They know how to read, all they do is lie."

The cartman's disillusionment is visually accentuated by the fact that at the same time as an off-screen voice expresses his train of thoughts, he is made to cross "La Place de l'Indépendance," Dakar's main circle and meant to be the symbol of a new era and new hopes. For lack of education, he momentarily shows nothing but an elementary and confused feeling of class consciousness, which is soon replaced by accusations directed towards more immediate and concrete scapegoats. "No, it is the other fellow's fault, the one with the dead child. If it were not for him, I would not be here. It is all his fault. And there was the griot, it is the griot's fault. Who cares if my ancestors were heroes? Now I am broke. What am I going to tell my wife? What will I tell her now? It was the same yesterday and the day before."

Discouraged while realizing the futility of his daily efforts, he continues lamenting about being imprisoned in a state of deprivation which he merely attributes to repeated bad luck. At no time does he seem to reflect upon the inadequacies of his trade. "It was the same yesterday and the day before. I work for nothing. What will I say when I get home? How will I pay for my cart now? All I can do is die."

His inability to support his family plunges him into deep despair. He is well aware that his economic impotence will affect his leadership as the head of a family unit. Since his social power as an African male is nullified, would death allow him to escape the shame his inadequacies bring upon him? He is psychologically castrated by his failures and is thus momentarily aspiring to the ultimate castration of death. Yet, the protagonist's grim outlook is tempered briefly as he is reintegrated into his familiar neighborhood. "This is my neighborhood, my village. Here I feel better. It is not like back there. Here there are no cops, nobody. We are among ourselves."

The alienated cartman reaches home. His cart has been confiscated. The absence of his main tool makes him more dispossessed at the close of his day than he was at its beginning and his social identity is at stake since "Borom Sarret," the name given to him by his customers, is no longer suitable. Here, as far as film techniques are concerned, Sembene takes great care in staging the composition of the subsequent pictures, illustrating the societal changes which are taking place within the family structure. In contrast to the beginning of the film, Fathma, lighting a fire to cook the evening meal, is highlighted. Through parallel action, the viewer is shown a quick full shot of the cartman slowly walking home. This is followed by a medium close-up of Fathma placing a big pot on the fire at the time she is expecting her husband's return. She does this with the child tied on her back, hoping that he will bring home the necessary ingredients for the evening meal. In the next scene, the cartman passes the threshold of his compound. He sadly tells her in a weary voice: "Don't expect a thing from me. I haven't even got my cart." Fathma does not chastise him with reproachful silent looks nor does she harass him with questions. The cartman sits in the circle marked with stones in which he ordinarily prays. Fathma quietly unties their child from her back and gives it to her husband, saying: "I promise you, we will eat tonight." Then she goes out turning away the two young children (*talibés*) who are begging for their marabout: "Go away, there is nothing here." Her voice reflects resignation and again no anger emanates from her statement. With their child in his arms, the cartman watches his wife exit and says to himself: "Where is she going? There is nothing to eat."

The last sequence of *Borom Sarret* emphasizes two different attitudes in response to a given situation. The cartman is left standing motionless within the praying circle which metaphorically represents tradition and religion imprisoning him. After his unsuccessful day, it is the place within which the cartman chooses to shelter himself. His wife, without consulting him, takes the initiative of going out with the firm belief that she will be able to provide some food for her household. One witnesses here a complete reversal of male and female roles within traditional African society. Usually, the man works outside and the woman stays at home to care for her house and family. The head of a family of modest income normally gives his wife the money required for the daily purchases of the household. In *Borom Sarret*, a man ill adapted to the demands of his urban setting, his cart more suited to a rural environment than to a city, loses his status. It is taken over by the woman, who, in addition to being a procreator and a protector, becomes a provider. Her motion and gestures stand in sharp contrast to her companion's inertia. She pragmatically leaves the family compound to earn money after her husband has collapsed in a state of fatalistic apathy. Some of the cartman's previous thoughts have indicated the repetition of such sterile days. His reaction to her decision, as well as her own resolution, may also reveal the frequency of such experiences.

With no specific skill, Fathma is left with little more than three opportunities to provide food for her family at the close of a day. She might depart to borrow money from obliging neighbors, but since lack of money is obviously general, this opportunity already may have been exhausted. She might go out to sell some of her personal belongings: a valuable necklace or bracelet. Yet, in this plot, the modesty of the family's life-style precludes such an alternative. Her last possibility is to obtain money through work. Considering her situation, one is led to the conclusion that her body might very well be the only marketable asset she possesses. *Borom Sarret* ends on Fathma's departure and the viewer is left to imagine where she goes. At this point, the spectator is expected to create his own film and provide his own ending. If prostitution is here envisioned, *Borom Sarret* lends itself to a tragic conclusion. Not only does the African woman take over her husband's prerogatives but she does so through selling her own body, the only marketable good she possesses in her extreme poverty. According to African and Muslim traditions, a wife belongs to her husband. As she is forced to prostitute herself to provide nourishment for their family, her action brings into sharp focus her husband's total dispossession.

Through the portrayal of the elderly merchant woman and that of the cartman's wife, Sembene also underlines the pragmatism and the abnegation of the traditional African woman when the survival of her family is at stake. In times of great need, she is prepared, at whatever cost, to provide the basic sustenance of her household.

In *Borom Sarret*, the resourcefulness of the cartman's wife and the elderly merchant woman contrasts with his own inadequacies. Yet one is also brought to believe that the protagonist's current deprivation is more linked to his awkward choice of an anachronistic trade in an evolving technocratic urban society than to his lack of enterprise or character. The cartman looks to be around thirty years old. His compound is simple but rather well built and well kept. Although a Muslim, he has only one wife, which might be explained by his circumstances. In this situation, his meager resources would not allow him to support a larger family and several spouses. Throughout the film, no hint is made as to close relatives who could be contacted in times of need as is often done in the extended African family—clearly an illustration of the social alienation suffered by many Senegalese families in urban areas. Only husband, wife, and child share the compound, thus pointing out that the cartman's roots are probably elsewhere and that he came recently to establish himself in Dakar, attracted by the mirage of opportunity offered by Senegal's main city. At various points in the film, he is very ill at ease having to face unfamiliar urban regulations. It is with deep relief that he will come back to his section of town, which he calls "his village." Although living on the outskirts of town, the term "village" might reveal his rural background.

Towards the end of the film, while handing his identity papers to the policeman, Borom Sarret's war medal drops on the street. This medal discloses other facets of his past. Since the action of *Borom Sarret* is situated in the early sixties, one might reasonably assume that the cart driver served in the French colonial army and performed an act of bravery. His age suggests that he was too young to participate in World War II but probably that he was in the French Army during the Indochina war. Displaced from his former background because of his military duties, he came back to his native country with some money after his army discharge. He subsequently married and decided to try his luck in Dakar, where he had enough money to build his compound and buy a horse to start his trade as a cartman. At that time, he selected an occupation which has a certain degree of independence and sought to succeed by himself and for himself. His failure derives from a shortsighted view of the profits he would obtain within a context plagued with poverty, as his customers are for the most part penniless. Lacking a basic education, trustful, and even naive, the cartman appears as the victim of a world he does not understand. His lack of a name in the film, where he is only alluded to through a name describing his trade, lends his character a collective social dimension: Sembene illustrates the painful problems resulting from a gap between tradition and modernism within the developing Senegalese society. The cartman, however, has mostly an individualistic and fatalistic perception of his dispossession, as Sembene makes him encounter others who are as deprived as himself, thus emphasizing the collective aspect of their condition. The cartman passes a man dutifully spinning in a most archaic way alongside a dirt road and later encounters small vendors at the marketplace. The young shoeshiner who picks a customer at the site of the griot's delivery is another outsider of Senegal's economic mainstream. The griot himself depends on the generosity of those poorer than himself. No longer country people but not yet full-fledged city dwellers, these people barely manage to survive on the outskirts of town. The squeaking, failing wheel of the cart symbolizes the uncertain dynamics of such world. This is stressed by Sembene through repeated and successive close-ups of the cart wheel and the horse's hoofs intermingled with long shots of swift modern cars.

With much skill and accuracy Sembene points out the disastrous effect of a lack of education, adequate training, and proper job opportunities for urban masses plagued with unemployment. He deplores such corrupting societal conditions which may lead men (at all levels) to steal and women to prostitute themselves and disrupt the cohesiveness and stability of the African family and moral values. "The beggars are like flies" sighs Borom Sarret, and their number reveals the yet insufficient socioeconomic measures taken by a nation which cannot effectively integrate its poor into the infrastructure of society. The one eye of the beggar metaphorically illustrates such social castration in a microcosm where everyone seems ready to exploit whoever is in a vulnerable position: the griot draws the cartman's last pennies in exchange for a vicarious escape into a glorious past, a man in a suit cheats the shoeshine boy during the griot's performance, and finally the cartman, entangled in police formalities, sees his customer leave without paying his fare. Such is, in *Borom Sarret*, Sembene's bitter and accusatory perception of the exploitative patterns and economic inadequacies of Senegal, problems which faith alone (religious faith as well as the man's faith to find work or the cartman's wife's faith to find food for her family) could hardly resolve.

NOTE

1. From an interview with Ousmane Sembene conducted by the author in Atlanta, 11 November 1979.

5
BLACK GIRL (1966): FROM BOOK TO FILM

Black Girl, like other films by Sembene such as *Niaye, Mandabi*, and *Xala*, is based on one of his written works. In adapting this short story, taken from *Voltaïque* (published in English under the title *Tribal Scars*), Ousmane Sembene rewrites the dialogue for the screen, combining the main elements of the original material in a compelling psychological drama, one of the masterpieces of early African cinema.[1]

Diouana, a Senegalese maid transplanted to France by her white employers, is the main character around whom both the short story and the film revolve. Her loneliness, exploitation, and humiliation lead her to commit suicide. This is her ultimate form of expression within the framework of linguistical alienation, psychological oppression, and dehumanization she has had to endure.

Originally, *Black Girl* was conceived as a seventy-minute feature film which included a color sequence illustrating Diouana's journey along the French Riviera after she has landed in France. The present version of *Black Girl* is limited to an hour. One cannot but regret the absence of the dramatic impact of the color sequence in the current print of Sembene's film. It emphasized the gap between the main protagonist's dreams and what she was about to experience during her subsequent stay in France.

The following pages focus on *Black Girl* as a case study exemplifying Sembene's skills in translating his sociopolitical aesthetics from literature into film. But before dealing with these transformations, it is of foremost importance to point out that the film is set during the first years of Senegal's independence, while the short story takes place during the last years of the French presence in Africa. In the book, Diouana's employer works for a French airline in Dakar while the film defines him as an advisor in the technical program provided by France to independent Senegal. The fact that the social comments made in the book can be maintained essentially unchanged in the film indicates that for Sembene, Senegal's present political and economic systems are identical to those of a colonized country. In Sembene's mind, Senegal's contemporary system is merely a prolongation of the prior colonial system. In both contexts, Senegal is kept dependent.

In Sembene's book, Diouana's alienation is more progressive than in his film. At the beginning of the short story, a certain dialogue exists between Diouana and the white couple who have hired her for modest wages in Dakar. She is able to communicate with them in the pidgin French spoken by some illiterate West African people. Her sentences, although short and clumsy, are more articulate than the limited "yes ma'ams" or "yes sirs" stammered by Diouana in the film. Here, her monosyllabic replies parallel, in a metaphorical manner, the sub-human condition to which she is reduced by her employers who are, in the film, also more condescending and one dimensional than in the short story. Sembene, however, re-establishes the necessary balance. Diouana cannot express herself in French but her thoughts are formulated to the viewer in French through the magic of the offscreen voice device. One has yet to emphasize that the use of French does harm to the authenticity of the film since Diouana is certainly not expected to think in French but rather in Wolof or some other African language spoken in Senegal, especially since she is illiterate (in 1965, less than 1 percent of women in Senegal were able to write or even to speak in French). In this instance, however, Sembene had to satisfy his French sponsors since *Black Girl* as well as *Borom Sarret* are Franco-Senegalese productions. As one pursues the comparison between the short story and the film, one notices that in the former, many characters interact and give their own version of the elements leading to Diouana's suicide. In the film, the focus remains on Diouana, but all the events are seen through her except, of course, the short scenes following her death. Thus, the spectator closely witnesses Diouana's fate through her own accounts and he is therefore better prepared to share her plight.

The short story is written in a style which could be compared to that of Chester Himes or Georges Simenon. It starts with the police investigation after Diouana's suicide and ends with an excerpt from a short article mentioning what is apparently the "unimportant" event of Diouana's suicide. The bulk of the short story relates the circumstances prior to her death from the viewpoint of both her employer and the narrator. Breaking away from the detective story approach, the film confronts the viewer with a more personal tone within the carefully structured pattern and heightened dramatic climaxes through pictures of great soberness.

It is undeniable that Sembene's experience as a writer has helped him to successfully achieve the various transformations usually required by screen adaptations of written works; for example, omission or reduction of lengthy passages from the book. Yet the excessive simplifications often found in Hollywood movies adapted from books and destined for mass consumption are avoided by Sembene, who trusts the viewer's intelligence. The film opens with a chronological account of Diouana's arrival in France. As her life unfolds there, an object or a particular situation reminds her of past occurrences through appropriate prolonged flashbacks.

To reach an optimum "unity of action" which fits the condensation of the prior material, Sembene has left out secondary characters, namely the sister and parents of Diouana's employer, the police investigators, the coroner, the medical expert, the neighbor (a retired sea captain), the photographer, and the journalists looking for sensationalism. In the written work, all these people are of minimal importance and their absence does not greatly alter the story. Samba, the cook at the French couple's Senegalese residence, is only briefly shown in the film, while he is given a more meaningful role in the story as the devoted and grateful servant of a white family. Also left out of the film is Tive Corréa, a drunken Senegalese veteran from the French Army who provides Diouana with some warnings as to her unrealistic expectations about France. The absence of Tive Corréa is compensated in the film by the creation of a new character, Diouana's boyfriend. It is he who expresses to Diouana the same dubious feelings as the veteran about her dreamlike vision of France. The French couple's children are reduced in number in the film and they do not show the same cruelty as in the book, where they occasionally sing derogatory songs about Diouana's skin color. Another transformation which takes place in the film is that of the white employers' domicile in France. In the book, the appropriately named "Hermitage Drive" leads Diouana to a secluded villa, similar to the one in which she lived in Dakar, while in the film it takes her to an apartment building. In the film, her living conditions undergo a more drastic change. She is confined to the limited space and anonymous condition of apartment dwellers. Here, her geographical as well as her spatial environment contribute to psychological and physical estrangement.

The additions noticed in *Black Girl* are very significant and provide the viewer with many visual symbols which are directly linked to the broader and more symbolical function given to Diouana. If Sembene inserts in his film Diouana's relationship with a young Senegalese bureaucrat, it is not to increase the romantic appeal of the story. Diouana remembers the young man as she looks at their picture in her lonely room. Sembene uses this snapshot as a transition between her life in Senegal and the one she is leading in France. She met the young man in the street. He was wearing a European suit while she was dressed in Senegalese attire. Immediately, clothing stressed the difference between the two characters. Although she lived on the outskirts of town, she had kept strong ties to the African tradition. He was more familiar with European culture and history which he had tended to adopt, although a portrait of the late Patrice Lumumba, one of Zaire's first leaders, revealed his commitment to African nationalism. This is seen later in the film when he gets angry and upset as Diouana, expressing her joy at going to France, naively proceeds to dance on the monuments to the dead Senegalese soldiers of the French Army, an attitude that derives more from ignorance than disrespect. It is also interesting to note that the young man, who is familiar with both African and European traditions, is indirectly responsible for Diouana's future connections with the French family. Since she is looking for a job, he sends her to the "maid market," a Dakar street corner where people come to choose and hire their help. This maid market is indeed reminiscent of a slave market. It is there that her future mistress comes to select her, while in the short story Diouana is hired through newspaper ads. Such a scene clearly has more graphic impact on the screen than would a simple transfer of the episode in the book. This symbolism is by no means accidental. Besides Diouana's own references to her enslavement in the film, the end of the short story includes a poem which draws a parallel between the condition of slaves and that of Diouana. Thus, one can really assert that the role of the young Senegalese goes beyond the "boy meets girl" dear to Hollywood. His main role is to complete Diouana's portrayal and reveal her to the viewer as a true-to-life character. She is not a sentimental vacuum but a grown-up woman with emotions and feelings. She is shown functioning normally within her own society. As a maid, not only will she become culturally alienated in a French environment, but she will also be reduced to the level of a subservient human being with stifled sexual drives.

Sembene also inserts in his film the sequence showing two Senegalese representatives as they leave the National Assembly. Their conversation discloses to the audience that their ambitions are essentially geared towards personal gains rather than the welfare of their constituency. Diouana passes them as she returns from a fruitless job-seeking trip in the wealthy Plateau district of Dakar. As she knocks at various doors, two little girls come running down the hall of an apartment building. One is black and the other is white. Both enjoy the same housing privileges. Through the two scenes depicting Diouana's encounters, Sembene demonstrates that the social gap he denounces is not so much between blacks and whites but rather between economic classes of people.

The scene in which Diouana's employers read the letter her mother is alleged to have written her is also absent in the short story. In this letter, her mother accuses Diouana of being ungrateful. She asks her for money to help support her family in Dakar. Although the request seems plausible, Diouana does not believe such a letter was sent by her mother. She thinks in anger: "It is not true. It is not my letter. This letter is not from my mother." Later in the film, the mother's reaction as she refuses the money from Diouana's employer conveys the impression that Diouana's doubts are well founded.

The filmmaker insists on Diouana's illiteracy as an important contributing factor in her alienation. Her employers try all possible means to convince her to work more efficiently. In so doing, they use the pretense of the letter to develop in her a sense of responsibility towards her family, thinking that this device will bring fruitful results. Yet their efforts are useless since Diouana feels increasingly exploited as well as odiously duped. She thinks: "I am their prisoner, Madame cheated me, now she will have to take care of her children." Finally, Diouana stays in her room and refuses to work, completing the physical isolation which will result in death.

In *Voltaïque*, there is mention of Diouana being "exhibited" by her employers to their friends and family. In *Black Girl*, Sembene creates a very meaningful sequence in which Diouana is requested to show her talents as a trained native and an exotic cook. During the meal, the conversation includes praises of her employers' lucrative and comfortable life in neo-colonial Dakar. One of the guests hopes that Diouana's cooking is an "aphrodisiac." Another insists upon kissing her. "Allow me to kiss you, miss, I have never kissed a nigger woman before." As Diouana's face shows her inner disgust and reluctance to do so, she hears the following insulting comment: "Since their independence, the niggers have lost a lot of their natural dispositions." So, besides her own comment upon Senegal's relationship with France, the filmmaker depicts the racist biases of the average Frenchman about Africans; for example, their alleged sexual endowment and lack of mental sophistication.

As a writer, Sembene starts his story by asserting the apathy and indifference of the leisured class lying in the sun on the French Riviera. The story takes place in 1958 and the people on the beach are far removed physically as well as psychologically from the social and political issues of their colonial possessions in Africa, although France is engaged in the Algerian war. As he changes the time period of his film, Sembene displaces and transforms the above-mentioned elements. After her suicide, Diouana's naked black body is shown lying in a bathtub filled with bloody water. A subsequent scene shows white people on the beach, eager to suntan and blacken their bodies. The action now takes place in the early sixties; the colonial turmoils have passed but one of the sunbathers casually reads the few lines in the paper devoted to Diouana's death with the same indifference previously noted in the story. He looks totally unaffected and untouched by the drama which took place in a nearby apartment building. Using the similarity of horizontal and naked bodies and a drastic contrast in color and location, Sembene gives more impact to his comment through the visual medium of the film than through the narrative rendition of his short story.

To supplement the significant alterations observed in Diouana's portrayal as it is transposed from book to film, it is interesting to analyze the title of the short story in French as compared to its translation in the English version of Ousmane Sembene's film. *La Noire de*, the title of both the short story and the film in French, literally means "The Black Girl Of." The preposition "of" indicates that she belongs to someone and although this person is not mentioned by name, Diouana depends on or is owned by someone. Here it is not the employer's name which matters but rather the class of people they represent. Whether she is the Smith's or the James's black girl, her existence as a maid depends on her masters. She is deprived of her own autonomy as an independent human being and she is known as someone's "black woman" or "black maid" rather than by her own name, as it is reflected in the title of the short story. Sembene expounds:

This black woman is someone who has been transplanted from her original environment. She no longer has a name. Before, she was not even aware of the fact that she was "black," with all the possible connotations associated with this word. She used to function adequately in her own surroundings. But once she left her country, she lost her identity as Diouana. She became somebody's black maid. She became an object belonging to a white family—their trophy.[2]

The English title of the film, *Black Girl*, which Sembene agreed to adopt, partly erases the above considerations (for instance, her "belonging" to someone) but equally deprives Diouana of her rights as an adult and alludes to her subservient status. Although she appears to be over twenty, she is not the "black woman" but rather the "black girl." This detail is reminiscent of the derogatory "boy" or "black boy" which was until quite recently commonly attributed by some whites to adult blacks in the United States. *La Noire de* as well as *Black Girl* can be associated with the servile position of a black maid in Africa, Europe, and elsewhere. The film, in which no mention of Diouana's origin is made (she is Diola and comes from Casamance in the book—the Diola maids represent a large part of the domestic workers in Dakar and are looked down upon by the Wolof), stresses the universal range of the plot. *La Noire de* could as well be translated as "the black woman from." Not only could she come from any region of Africa, but from any region of the world. Her problems not only derive from her race but from her social condition and could be those of a Spanish maid working for a French family or those of a Latin American domestic in the United States.

The camera has the matchless capability of emphasizing details, and Sembene uses this to stress the symbolic impact of certain objects (added to the film) and their significance in relation to its main character. As she starts working for the French family, Diouana covers the braids of her African hairdo with a wig made of straight hair. She now espouses European standards of beauty. As the film progresses, she wears the used high-heeled shoes and old European clothes given to her by her employer. She adopts the look of a transitional African woman setting foot in the Western world. In France, her employer attributes her resentful attitude to her arrogance. As Diouana wears her used belongings, her mistress is critical of her look—too much like her own—which in her mind does not correspond to that of a docile African servant. For her, Diouana's summer dress and high heels negate the submissiveness which is supposed to be linked to her social status. She demands that Diouana wear sandals and an apron while performing her domestic duties. Diouana soon reacts to such daily humiliations and mistreatments. From having begun as a babysitter in Senegal, she is now a live-in maid and cook in France. She ponders: "Madame won't tell me anymore to go and do the laundry. I shall never be a slave. I did not come to France for the apron and the money. She will never see me again. Never will anyone tell me anything. Madame lied to me. She has always lied to me. She will no longer lie to me. She wanted to keep me here like a slave."

As she carefully gathers her belongings and puts them in a suitcase, Diouana discards her European dress and wig. Naked, with her hair braided the African way, Diouana lies in the bathtub and cuts her throat with her employer's razor. In his short story, Sembene has Diouana's body, hidden by a cover, removed from her employer's house by two stretcher bearers. In the film, Sembene prefers to show the last shot of Diouana soon after she commits suicide. A few scenes later, the filmmaker presents us with a close-up of the bathtub thoroughly cleaned, bearing no visible trace of the maid's tragic end. In the white world her death is washed away, but, as will be seen, her memory will remain forever alive in her former Arican community.

The major element added by Sembene to his film is an African mask which, like her boyfriend's picture, takes her mind back to Africa and reveals certain aspects of her personality. In Dakar after being hired, Diouana is not ill treated according to the rules which seem to govern the relationship between employers and servants. The French woman behaves rather kindly towards her, perhaps due to the fact that the young French woman is herself an alien in an environment which is familiar to Diouana. To show her appreciation, Diouana gives her a mask purchased from her little brother.

The mask is a symbol of friendship and trust on Diouana's part. Removed from its original setting (communal ceremonies), based on a monetary exchange, and offered for purposes other than a religious ritual, the mask has already been perverted and loses its primary function within the African tradition. For Diouana's employers, who own several African art objects, the mask is nothing more than a new acquisition for their collection (they are not interested in African art but rather in the money it represents). As the mask is hung on their wall, it goes through a second desecration. It is now static and dead in so far as it is no longer used in traditional African ceremonies. Later, the mask becomes a symbol of discord between Diouana and her employers. As they betrayed her trust, she vehemently claims it back. Before she commits suicide, Diouana puts it with her belongings. After her death, the husband brings it back to Diouana's mother. Then the mask is taken back by Diouana's little brother. He puts it on his face and proceeds to walk slowly behind Diouana's former employer. The latter hastens his pace while crossing the iron bridge which leads from the slums to one of Dakar's main roads. The mask worn by the little boy becomes a new symbol of Africa, past and present. It follows the white man's guilt and eventually rejects him. Earlier in the film, the little boy has been seen playing with a toy he fabricated out of dumped wheels. He has already inserted modern technology in his games but at the same time he associates himself with the traditional African mask. Here the spectator might perhaps reflect that it is through similar symbiosis that Africa will assert itself in the future. The last scene of the film, showing Diouana's belongings being taken back to her family, provides the viewer with a strikingly silent confrontation between Diouana's mother and her former employer in which the feelings of dejection and relentless pride of a traditional African woman are superbly expressed. Sembene explains how he came to include this scene in his film.

I could have ended my film with Diouana's suicide. I added the white man's return to Africa to show how we are killed and how the culprits remain unpunished. One does not only kill people's bodies but their minds. The white employer has been shown as a hunter with all his African art objects. These are people who kill Africa. I had to show how neo-colonialism kills us. Beyond the suicide of a young woman transplanted to another region, one has to see that the man responsible for her suicide went back to Africa. Is he going to hire another maid? I had to show people that the issue is not to commit suicide but to fight because colonialism is not over.[3]

It is also significant to point out that the passing along of the African mask is accompanied by songs of lament which replace the poem dedicated to Diouana's memory in the short story. Through the little boy, Sembene puts the mask back into motion and its bearer becomes permeated and transformed by its power. The songs which are simultaneously heard create the atmosphere of a symbolized funeral ceremony. The last picture of the film is a close-up of the little boy withdrawing his mask. He now faces the audience with a bare face and a sustained look. It announces the determination of the young Senegalese generations who will evolve within but also beyond the traditional African values embodied in the mask. As he introduces the mask in *Black Girl*, Sembene includes in his film an extremely significant symbol for the non-visual concepts of trust, sorrow, and the very incarnation of the proud spirit of Diouana. The end of this film is like a manifesto: the haunting mask reflects Africa's determination to search in its traditions the strength of liberating itself from Western tutelage.

Comparing books to their Hollywood screen adaptations, Lester Asheim observes:

The tone of negation is never retained completely in the adaptation of a novel to the screen. Although more than half of the "unhappy" endings are retained in the sample films, none of them keeps the note of indecision, frustration, hopelessness, or despair which marks the novels. In every instance action is rearranged or rewritten to provide hope and consolation, a sense of pattern and meaning, and a note of affirmation.[4]

Later, in that same article, Lester Asheim points out that "if evil goes unpunished or good unrewarded in the novel, the film changes the plot to show the concrete punishment of evil and at least the promise of reward to goodness."[5]

In *Black Girl*, although not a Hollywood film, the last sequence added to the film eradicates some of the negative tone found in the short story. Considering Sembene's writing and filmmaking, one can assume that he did not do so to please his audience or respond to outside pressures. Diouana's death is placed in a broader context than in the short story, where her death appears simply as the tragic consequence of an individual destiny. The film indicates that Diouana lives on through the mask which becomes a memorial figure ensuring her immortality. Having entered the ancestors' world, she remains in constant contact with the terrestrial cycle of life and influences it, as is believed in many African religions.

The memory of Diouana's pains is shared by her former neighbors and extended into the future through the mask reclaimed by her little brother, who assumes the role of a reliquary guardian figure. Sembene elects to interpret the role of the schoolteacher who leads her employer through her former neighborhood. He is a link between the Western world and the African tradition. As a modern literate griot, he is the recorder of facts who tells Diouana's former neighbors: "Folks, this is Diouana's boss." Through a succession of close-ups of their faces, the camera lingers on their tense looks and contained anger. There is an unmistakable tension, but Sembene willingly discards any physical confrontation between the Africans and the white man. He explains that, "at this point, it would have been easy but unrealistic to have the white man killed by the Africans. . . . In a creative work, it is difficult to have people take a gun and kill whites. Had we done this in real life all over Africa, would whites have left Africa?"[6]

In *Black Girl*, Sembene's plot goes beyond Diouana without impoverishing her as a character. Diouana's alienation starts when she leaves her neighborhood to work in the residential section of Dakar. It grows into silent rebellion after her passage from Africa to France, when her ancillary humiliation is increased by her alienation as an African expatriate. Diouana's alienation culminates in her death. Since suicide is infrequent in most African societies, it emphasizes her cultural estrangement. Yet this negative aspect of Diouana's death is redeemed by the filmmaker as her mask is taken back to her people. Thus, her experience becomes a part of their common history. Sembene rejects heroes who are essentially individualistic in nature. He remarks:

If you take a child and send him on some errands, and if you film him from the moment he leaves to the moment he comes back, this child becomes a hero. Yet as he comes back from his errands, he comes back within his community and goes back to the person who sent him shopping. The myth of the hero is a European creation. The so-called protagonist has no meaning if she or he is taken out of the community.[7]

From the printed word to the moving picture, Sembene has heightened the dramatic impact of his original narrative, while artfully illustrating the most significant steps of Diouana's itinerary, which he enhances with a broader symbolic value. Through the last sequence of the film, Diouana's suicide—self-aggression but also her ultimate means of expression—brings a collective awareness and as such is more meaningful than in the short story.

Diouana's death is indeed seen by Sembene as the soil which will nourish future action against the present exploitative status quo existing between so many Africans, their former colonial rulers, and their neo-colonial successors. Through Diouana, as well, the filmmaker warns his compatriots about the chimerical, dreamlike vision they may have of France and denounces the dark mirror of emigration.

NOTES

1. Sembene Ousmane, *Tribal Scars* (London: Heinemann, 1974).
2. From an interview with Ousmane Sembene conducted by the author at Howard University, Washington, D.C., 19 February 1978.
3. From a lecture delivered by Ousmane Sembene at Howard University, 21 March 1975.
4. Lester Asheim, "From Book to Film," *The Quarterly of Film, Radio and Television*, vol. 6, n. 3 (1952), p. 264.
5. Ibid.
6. Sembene's lecture, Howard University, 1975.
7. Ibid.

6
MANDABI (1968): ILLITERACY VERSUS BUREAUCRACY

Mandabi, whose title means "this money order" in Wolof, is a comedy of character, situation, and manners with deep social overtones. It takes place in Dakar less than a decade after the independence of Senegal, in a world in transition from agrarian poverty to the poverty of industrialism, capitalism, and consumerism. It shows what money "orders" and the perils which may befall a simple man with "sudden money" in such a society. The film, made in 1968, is Sembene's first color feature film and describes the quixotic adventures of Ibrahima Dieng, a pompous but poor man, as he sets out to cash a money order from his nephew. His efforts are balked by bureaucracy and dishonesty. At the end of the story, he is more in debt and poorer than ever. In Sembene's terms:

> He is caught in a situation that goes beyond him because he has always thought that he was, as Ibrahima Dieng, a personality in his neighborhood where everybody knows him. But as he goes out of his own traditional culture, he goes to a modern culture where the identity card has nothing to do with internal autonomy within a group where he was not an anonymous person. Out of his culture, he becomes an anonymous person. In this context, identity papers are needed. Identity papers are created by laws, and laws sometimes create the most dishonest people. In the final analysis, the one who

stole the money order did not actually steal it as far as laws are concerned. Ibrahima gave him the power of attorney in order to cash it. According to law, one is able to transfer such prerogatives. Yet one cannot foresee whether this person will not use such prerogatives in a devious way. Whenever laws exist, embezzlements are possible. I don't mean that it does not exist without laws, but a law allows educated people to "legally" exploit uneducated people.[1]

According to Ousmane Sembene, *Mandabi* was primarily geared to Senegalese audiences. "The thing I was trying to do in it was to show Africans some of the deplorable conditions under which they themselves live. When one creates, one does not think of the world: one thinks of one's country. It is, after all, the Africans who will ultimately bring about change in Africa—not the Americans, or the French or the Russians or the Chinese."[2]

It often happens, however, that the impact of a work of art exceeds the intentions of its author. This has been precisely the case for *Mandabi*, considered by many critics as the first African film able to reach worldwide audiences. The appeal of this internationally praised motion picture is due not only to its universal significance but also to its style, which has—except for one flashback and the editing of the final sequence—an uncomplicated narrative tying together the repeated mishaps of Ibrahima's search. Sembene's approach is ironic but never patronizing. His camera is at ease among the people he knows so well. He is attentive to the manners of ordinary Senegalese people when they eat, drink, sleep, or wash themselves. *Mandabi* does not have unexpected climaxes or elaborate camera effects but has nonetheless a very sustained drama. Some observers, like Margaret Tarratt, have been struck by the static and theatrical qualities of this film. According to her:

It relies heavily for interest on the virtuoso performance of the elderly Ibrahima, strutting but ingenuous, who moves through the city streets with his ample robes billowing impressively like some fat exotic bird puffing out feathers. The theatrical quality may be the result of the film's un-cinematic structure of a rigid and predictable plot worked out in terms of a number of small scenes which are always played out to their conclusion.[3]

Mandabi, based on Sembene's story of the same name, is enjoyably fresh yet often bitterly caustic. But, as it details a relentless journey in the labyrinth of the absurd, its theme also evokes distress and anguish. In spite of its stylistic appeal, however, *Mandabi* is more sociological, moral, and philosophical than purely cinematic. In it, the filmmaker delineates the impact of a money economy, in a developing nation, on interpersonal relationships according to social strata.

Ibrahima Dieng's ordeal begins with the notice for a money order which the mailman brings to his house while he is absent from his family compound. The money order is sent to Ibrahima by his nephew who is now working in France because in his own words, "There is no work in Dakar."[4] The money order amounts to $100 and of this sum $80 is to be saved by Ibrahima for his nephew's return, $12 must be given to the nephew's mother (Ibrahima's sister) and $8 for Ibrahima because the nephew knows he is unemployed and needs help. Ibrahima's allotment is indeed quite small even by 1968 standards, and the expectations it arouses seem disproportionate to its size.

Ibrahima's final loss of the money order is made even more dramatic by our knowledge of how it has been earned. Through off-screen voice, we learn about the nephew's arduous work as a street sweeper and his striving for a better life by attendance at night school. This voice is that of a public writer to whom Ibrahima has come to have his nephew's letter read because he himself is illiterate. As the public writer reads the letter, a flashback sequence shows a close-up of the broom which Ibrahima's nephew, Abdou, puts against the wall of a post office which he enters to mail the money order, the key element of this film. Then Abdou is seen sweeping the Champs Elysées sidewalk at the end of which stands the Arc de Triomphe—a symbol that is in sharp contrast to Abdou's menial tasks. Other scenes of Paris, including its elevated metro system, fulfill two functions. The mythical evocation of Paris through its monuments, past glories, and technological achievements sheds lights on Abdou's social alienation in a context which remains dreamlike for many Africans. Furthermore, it indicates the alien aspect of the money order which comes from a society drastically different from Ibrahima's. From the beginning of the film, it is visually suggested that the money order comes from a foreign economy and that it brings with it the rules of its bureaucracy. At the same time, Sembene emphasizes that independent Senegal has kept intact the administrative system inherited from the French during colonial times. The key to such a system is reserved to an elite, those who speak French, a language Ibrahima neither understands nor speaks, thus rendering him powerless and exposed. Not knowing French, Ibrahima is completely separated and alien to the world this language reflects. Again, one must stress that it is the prospect of money rather than money itself which is the catalyst of Ibrahima's tribulations, initiating a spatial and social displacement into the unknown spheres of a bureaucratic world. In such a process of events, Ibrahima will face three stages of economy: that of his household, his neighborhood, and the modern inner city.

At first, Ibrahima Dieng is shown at home assuming his patriarchal functions. Although unemployed, he appears as a potbellied, bloated, domestic lord who rudely imposes his rule over his two wives (Mety and Aram) and his seven children, who all live in the same modest compound on the outskirts of town. Mety and Aram serve him, massage his feet, and run at the first blink of their master's eye. Yet the two co-wives work as a team and seem happy enough to share the burden of their daily routines. One has the feeling that, based on a perfect division of labor, all is well in the best polygamous world. Asked about *Mandabi* in terms of his own position concerning polygamy, Sembene answered, "I am against polygamy but my concern was not to deal with this subject in this film. Its unity of action would have suffered from it."[5]

All powerful at home, rushing his wives to prayer and domestic tasks as he wakes up from taking his afternoon nap, Ibrahima does not at first arouse the viewer's sympathy. However, his authority over his household is soon affected by the news of the forthcoming money.

"Don't talk about money in the street," says Ibrahima to one of his wives as she runs up to him to announce the mailman's notice for the money order. From the start, he fears the repercussion such information may have from his neighbors, friends, and relatives. Ibrahima's warning comes too late since his wife has already obtained needed rice on credit from the corner grocery, telling the shopkeeper of her husband's forthcoming good fortune. This news, conveyed by the Moorish grocer, is soon spread throughout the neighborhood. Displeased and angry, Ibrahima feels that his family authority has been by-passed and tells Mety and Aram that "good wives must wait for their husband's decision before doing anything. Now everybody, everybody will know that I have a money order."

It is as husband and father that Ibrahima succeeds best in exerting his traditional prerogatives, as long as his compound remains largely isolated from the outside world. With the coming of the money order, however, the sheltered aspect of his compound cannot be sustained and Ibrahima's last sanctuary is desecrated. The mailman passes the threshold of his house, establishing a link with modernity which cannot be avoided. Two cameos are introduced by Sembene in his film to prove that modern ways permeate even the closest, best-protected environments. One shows a long shot of a street vendor who slips into Ibrahima's compound. He carries a stick to which nylon brassieres are hanging like flags. One of Ibrahima's wives surrenders to the temptation of buying this cheap accessory of Western elegance. She is penniless but promises to pay for her purchase as soon as her husband's money order is cashed. It is to be remembered that Ibrahima had positively forbidden such deferred payment purchases and now once again his authority is transgressed. Living in a traditional setting, Ibrahima and his wives wear the long African gowns called boubous. The whole family speaks only Wolof and is illiterate. The only relationship they seem to have is with their neighbors in the Muslim community in which they live. Yet, the peddler's access to Ibrahima's home comes as a proof of the unavoidable and irreversible appeal of Western ways to Senegalese women.

The other cameo, is a short medium shot of one of Ibrahima's little girls playing with a white baby doll which she bathes in a plastic wash basin. In so doing, the little girl already practices her future role as a mother with a "made in France" celluloid offspring with which she cannot racially identify and by which she is invited to step in the world of Western consumerism. She also uses a basin and not the traditional calabash. This is explained by the fact that Ibrahima's family, although isolated, lives in an urban setting where such utensils can be purchased from a nearby market. Beyond the casual, everyday feature of a little girl playing with her doll, Sembene's camera stresses the pervasive and culturally alienating impact of Western industry through the intrusion of the white doll in Ibrahima's world.

The economy of the family's neighborhood is as precarious as that of its household. There also, apart from the relative affluence of the grocer and his friends, money is scarce. Trade is performed by peddlers (the brassiere seller and the water vendor) and retail dealers like the Moorish grocer. The grocer in question has a small, dark shop cluttered with varied local and imported goods, including rice from Asia—a comment on the absurdity of such procedure while large amounts of local Casamance rice are being exported. His backyard is used for various transactions, such as the pawning of items like Mety's gold necklaces at usurious rates of interest. On one occasion, the shopkeeper serves as intermediary for one of his customers who, aware of Ibrahima's debts, would like to purchase his house. This proposal is vehemently rejected by Ibrahima, who clings to his sole concrete asset, swearing he would rather die than part with his house. His attitude demonstrates his attachment to traditional measures of value such as land and house.

The money order disrupted the hierarchy of Ibrahima's household and also has a significant impact on relationship with his friends, immediate neighbors, and relatives. In many instances they initially respect him, but this turns to disdain. The grocer becomes obsequious when he first learns about the money order and proposes to reserve his most exclusive brand of rice for Ibrahima. He then lends him twenty cents for transportation, probably hoping to compensate himself by selling the rice. But later, as Ibrahima faces more and more difficulties in cashing his money order, the same grocer refuses to lend him more money and suggests the selling of his house. The two men then come to blows, the first of two physical confrontations Ibrahima has to endure because of the money order. The neighbors also suddenly prey on Ibrahima. The imam comes to him and says: "Life is hard today and I need your help. I need 5,000 francs C.F.A. [$20]." Dejected at the negative reaction he incurs, the imam does not hesitate to build up a lie to discredit Ibrahima by telling people: "I saw him handling a bundle of money. His wives run the household. There is no more solidarity." Other similarly parasitic friends plead with the co-wives for help. They say: "Mety, think about my wife and children who are hungry." When Mety is reluctant to give rice, the friend exclaims: "Allah protect us from domineering women." Before leaving the compound, he turns toward Ibrahima Dieng saying: "Don't let your wife lead you astray. A man should be a man!" Ibrahima's status as master of the household is jeeringly questioned and challenged by his peers. Yet Ibrahima's wives continue to oppose his generosity (and also authority) as he keeps insisting upon satisfying his neighbors' rapaciousness with their scarce family food supply for status' sake. Using a Wolof adage, they advise each other as follows: "We must get rice, we only have rice for three days. From now on, we won't give or lend anything. Give to nine poor people and you'll be the tenth."

As the story progresses, Ibrahima discovers at his expense that one does not cash a money order the same way one deals at the marketplace or with local shopkeepers. In his neighborhood, Ibrahima is known by name and can buy goods on credit. His word is sufficient and no signature is required. Downtown, anonymity is the rule and no one will acknowledge his existence without proof of it (identity card). Ibrahima has now to "legitimize" his identity. His word becomes worthless and each of his transactions has to be signed to be legal and identifiable. In the film, since Ibrahima is unable to write, he signs with a cross. Here, Sembene stresses that such signature leads back to the same impersonality this procedure is meant to defeat.

In order to find out his nephew's instructions about the money order, Ibrahima goes to a public writer who is seated at the back of the post office (an old colonial building). Then, when he goes to the post office window to cash the money order, the clerk asks for an identity card, which Ibrahima does not have. His friend, who is just as unaware as Ibrahima of what an identity card represents, proposes to lend his. The postal clerk tells Ibrahima that the money order will be kept for two weeks at the post office. In the meantime, he advises him to go to his local police station to obtain the necessary papers. As the public writer sees Ibrahima leave without paying him, he grabs Ibrahima's arm and insults him.

To go to the police station (another building of the colonial era), Ibrahima has to walk through the busy streets and sidewalks of Dakar. He is shown in long shots to emphasize the anachronism of his traditional clothing in a modern context. At the police station, a polite but condescending bureaucrat tells him that a birth certificate, three photographs, and a fifty francs C.F.A. (twenty cents) tax stamp are necessary to obtain an identity card.

At the city hall, another colonial edifice, where he goes to obtain a birth certificate, Ibrahima has to wait in line until the clerk has finished his conversation with a colleague about their practice of fraudulent checks. A customer has to read the papers Ibrahima is showing. Since they stipulate only that Ibrahima was born around 1900 in Dakar, the clerk refuses to issue the requested birth certificate for lack of certainty of the day of birth.

Confused, Ibrahima goes then to seek the help of one of his nephews, an educated young man who lives in a middle-class residential neighborhood. After Ibrahima states the reason for his visit, the nephew gives him some change and a check to cover the expenses incurred by the formalities through which he has to go. The nephew takes him to the city hall where he gets in touch with one of his acquaintances. He gives him the same information previously provided by Ibrahima concerning his birthdate. The clerk assures the nephew that the requested birth certificate will be ready the following day. In this short sequence, Sembene flashes a direct attack at the nepotism which, he maintains, is endemic among Senegalese civil servants.

On his way to the bank to cash his nephew's check, Ibrahima is approached by a young woman carrying a baby in her arms and begging. She says to him: "For the love of Allah, come to my aid." Following his Muslim custom of giving alms as he did before when a beggar came to his house, Ibrahima helps her. He gives her some change, adding: "May Allah's blessings be on you." As he walks towards the bank, Ibrahima hopes that his generosity will mark the end of the innumerable difficulties he has had to face until that point. He thinks to himself: "And may I be spared from evil and mishaps from now on." At this instant, the given coins possess a magical power and are perceived as protective amulets.

In front of the bank (a recently erected modern building), Ibrahima hesitates before entering. Noticing his behavior, a man in European clothes tells him he can arrange for him to cash the check without the customarily requested identity card. Indeed, shortly after the man has talked to the bank teller, Ibrahima is able to cash 1,000 francs C.F.A. ($4). Yet as he leaves the building, that "helpful" man, turned usurer/money changer asks for 300 francs C.F.A. ($1.20) for services rendered, alleging the bribe is for the teller and shamelessly adding: "The cost of living is high and he has a family to support."

Outraged by this experience, Ibrahima resumes his walk only to be approached by the same woman, who invents a new story to get money from him. He recognizes her and becomes angry at her nerve and arrogance. Realizing that she will not get anything more, the sycophant becomes angry in her turn and acts as though she was the injured party, shouting: "Don't you proposition me. I am a decent woman." After this, Sembene has his protagonist muse (having now forgotten his own prior solicitations): "Begging has become a profession. Where is the country going?"

Through this woman, Sembene illustrates once more the deprivation of lower-class Senegalese women who, out of necessity, have to adopt the traditionally male role of supporter of the family. She is shrewd and alert, using her status as a woman to reprimand Ibrahima. She does this in such a manner that if passersby were to overhear this altercation, Ibrahima's honesty and motives would be questioned. Ibrahima is well aware of this and has no choice but to leave. Sembene indicates here that the exploitation of Ibrahima in the inner city is not only the privilege of the literate elite but of anyone who is used to the city's ways. Such observation will be confirmed through Ibrahima's dealings with a local photographer.

In need of three photos for his identity card, Ibrahima goes to have pictures made. The photographer promises the photos will be ready the next day and requests a full advance payment of 300 francs C.F.A. ($1.20). The following day, Ibrahima goes three times to the photo shop. The third time he is told that the pictures did not come out and that he will not be reimbursed (in a previous sequence, the viewer has witnessed the photographer's dishonesty as he took a picture without loading his camera). Again, Ibrahima engages in a physical confrontation with the photographer and their tiff draws a crowd of passersby who halt the fight. He is then seen, stooping on the sidewalk with blood dripping from his face. Morally and physically wounded, Ibrahima's distress at this new fraud causes him to say to himself with bitter resignation: "In a country like this, only scoundrels live well." Staggering, Ibrahima comes back to his compound. To cover up for this new defeat and protect him from further predatory intent, his wives shout repeatedly: "They've robbed him of the money."

Nine days have passed and the money order has not yet been cashed. To hasten the transaction, Ibrahima goes to see a broker he met after his scuffle at the grocery. The broker, whom the viewer has seen showing Ibrahima's house to a prospective client, has implied he could help him. The broker goes with Ibrahima to the police station to make him sign a power of attorney in his favor. Then the broker informs Ibrahima he has to leave on account of a business appointment and suggests that he should come back to see him the next day. So, as decided, Ibrahima goes to the broker's house to learn not only that the money has been cashed, but that the money allegedly has been stolen from the broker, who flatly explains: "I was the victim of pickpockets." Ibrahima is indignant and disbelieving, but the broker denies his allegations, swearing: "I'm not an infidel or a thief. I am a true believer." Ibrahima implores the broker's pity, explaining that he is not the sole beneficiary of the money order but merely acting as intermediary. Imperturbable, the broker is not sensitive to Ibrahima's pleas. We remember that Ibrahima's complete bankruptcy will facilitate the selling of the house for which the broker has a pending customer. He calls for one of his servants to give Ibrahima a bag of rice and takes him home in his car. After Ibrahima has been dropped off near his house, women rush towards him for a share of the rice until his wives come to his rescue by driving the predatory neighbors away. Back to his compound, Ibrahima feels more defeated and dispossessed than ever and swears: "I am going to become a wolf among wolves, a thief, a beggar." At this very moment the mailman enters the house with another letter from Paris. He tells Ibrahima not to lose hope in a brighter future.

Mailman: We will change the country.
Ibrahima: Who?
Mailman: You.
Ibrahima: Me?
Mailman: You, your wives, your children, and I will change it.

The mailman's comforting words provide little relief for Ibrahima. Sitting down, he thinks of all the events generated by the money order. Simultaneously, a succession of quick shots representing some of the most significant scenes from the film are flashed onto the screen before a medium shot if Ibrahima, who concludes with resignation: "Honesty is a sin in this country." Ibrahima Dieng has experienced the collapse of the safe and somewhat naive values of his restricted universe and has become the victim of corrupt bureaucrats and unscrupulous businessmen.

At the conclusion of *Mandabi*, Ibrahima's search has soared to an obsessive level. According to Jacques Aumont and Sylvie Pierre, it derives from the "conflict between the abstract idea of money . . . as it is conceived in consumer societies, and the materiality of wealth, as it is understood in an exchange economy."[6]

In *Mandabi*, the economic structures which result from Senegal's recent colonial administration are set up by the literate elite and remain alien to unsophisticated people who, possessing little, are totally ignorant of the workings of money in bank or postal operations. If this film contrasts two drastically different market economies and segments of societies at various levels of technological development, it also stresses the uncertain stability of an urban economy within which money is obtained through begging and all types of intermediary services.

Besides this dualism (reflected in buildings, clothing, behavior, and so on), *Mandabi* presents an in-depth reflection on the very nature and function of money. Here more than anywhere else, money is all powerful and acquires a supreme value. It generates power and respect for the wealthy and impotence and contempt for the poor. In this film, there are few characters to whom total honesty and integrity might be attributed. Money belittles moral and social values based on the traditional African ethic of mutual aid and solidarity. It becomes surrounded with devotion, deals, false promise, extortion, and dreams.

The money order notice has the power of disrupting the order of Ibrahima's value system and cultural microcosm. It is a sign of wealth, the symbol of a treasure with a key unknown to Ibrahima. Yet it has an invisible and impalpable force that the hero will never grasp (literally as well as figuratively). Coming from another world—both from a different geographical area and a society at a distinct stage of evolution—the money order (a piece of paper whose Latin characters are like inscrutable hieroglyphs to Ibrahima) becomes endowed with magic and maleficent powers. In such a respect, the money order is acquiring fetishistic qualities and becomes the medium between the untouchable money it symbolizes and the visual effects it spawns.

Because of a money order from which he will not profit, Ibrahima discovers that money can't buy happiness. Except for his protective and helpful wives, his compassionate nephew and his sympathetic mailman, Ibrahima is now despised by everybody he knows. The victim of a world he does not understand, Ibrahima becomes an existential and isolated anti-hero, ill equipped to function in a modern society. Yet however dispossessed, he is no longer under any illusion about human integrity. His naive dreams about honesty have been destroyed. At the end of the film, Ibrahima is more heavily in debt than ever but such poverty is largely compensated by his new knowledge of the corruption of bureaucrats and of his own vulnerability. His search is by no means sterile. Seeking his past (through his efforts to obtain a birth certificate) and his image (his attempts to get a photograph), he has undergone an initiatory ritual which brings him the wealth of practical wisdom he sorely needs.

In following Ibrahima, one notices that he is looking for a conciliation between ideals and a life which has become chaotic to him because of its alien characteristics. He experiences the disruption which has occurred in his coherent mythic-like vision of the world. With anguish, he somewhat perceives the conflicting dualism which exists between the bureaucratic, exploitative elite and people like himself. But such a feeling is tempered by the coming of the mailman who assures him of a future coherence of the myth. The mailman becomes the messenger of a new era which will restore order in an incongruous world. Linked to Ibrahima's misfortunes because he brought to him the money order notice, the mailman is now transformed into a bearer of hope, a vengeful but optimistic archangel who believes in the collective efforts of people to restore honesty and moral values as he tells Ibrahima: "We will change the country." In a Brechtian manner, the mailman's collective optimism culminates in a revolutionary prophecy. Ibrahima is no longer imprisoned in helplessness, he is now being initiated in political awareness in the hope of an egalitarian and equitable society. According to Margaret Tarratt:

> Sembene has said that in this film he denounces "in a Brechtian manner" the dictatorship of the bourgeoisie over the people. The bourgeoisie in this case are the petty officials, the small scale nouveaux riches marked out by their European dress, furnitures and cars all expressive of middle class aspiration. These people have woven a mesh of red tape in order to benefit themselves and to batter off the unsophisticated.[7]

Ibrahima's inability to cope with the red tape of the administrative framework is, in essence, an indictment of Senegal's failure to educate and to inform its common people. Yet the final message conveyed by Sembene in *Mandabi* is hopeful in spite of the many tragic facets of Ibrahima's story. Satirically denouncing the arrogance, nepotism, and exploitative traits of some of Senegal's bureaucrats, Sembene's motion picture ends with his customary trust in the capacity of the common people to work towards their own salvation.

NOTES

1. From a series of interviews with Ousmane Sembene conducted by the author in Senegal in 1978.
2. Guy Flatley, "Senegal Is Senegal, Not Harlem," *New York Times* (2 November 1969), p. D17.
3. Margaret Tarratt, "The Money Order," *Films and Filming*, vol. 20, n. 4 (1974), p. 48.
4. As he did in *Black Girl*, Sembene repeats here his criticism of Senegalese emigration to France, a reflection of Senegal's inability to make a complete use of its manpower, especially unskilled urban youth. According to *Africa Report*, (May–June 1969), more than half (13,000) of the 25,000 workers from black Africa in France are Senegalese. Here, only the proportion of Senegalese workers in relation to African workers can be considered accurate since these official figures do not include the many undocumented black African workers who were actually in France in 1969. In 1980, there were about 30,000 Senegalese workers in France (still half the number of black African workers in France). Again, with the number of illegal Senegalese migrants, the total number of Senegalese laborers is probably anywhere between 40,000 and 50,000 people, that is to say about 1 percent of Senegal's population.
5. Guy Hennebelle and Catherine Ruelle, "Cinéastes d'Afrique Noire," *L'Afrique Littéraire et Artistique*, n. 49 (1978), p. 177. Author's translation.
6. Jacques Aumont and Sylvie Pierre, "Huit Fois Deux," *Cahiers du Cinéma*, n. 206 (1968), p. 30. Author's translation.
7. Margaret Tarratt, "The Money Order," p. 45.

7
EMITAI (1971): MYTHS, TRADITIONS, AND COLONIALISM

The style of *Emitai*, a color, feature-length film, wavers between epic and documentary. In it, Ousmane Sembene shows his inveterate faith in the teachings of history. "We must understand our traditions before we can hope to understand ourselves."[1] He suggests that such traditions should be eliminated or altered when they hamper progress. Here, not only religion or colonialism are at stake, but anything that may weaken, debase, or corrupt Africa and delay its evolution. Defiantly, it is "to all the militants of the African cause" that the Senegalese filmmaker dedicates his film.[2]

Emitai, whose title means "god of thunder" in Diola, was practically entirely made in that language to emphasize the cultural distinctiveness of Sembene's story. Shot in seven weeks in the village of Dimbering, the action is set during World War II in Casamance, the most fertile region of Senegal, located south of the Gambia river. The plot of the film describes the French occupying forces, brutally forcing the villagers into military service, leaving only the elders, women, and children to safeguard the tribe and work their precious rice crop. *Emitai* details the rebellion of this village controlled by ancient

Chapter adapted from Françoise Pfaff, "Myths, Traditions and Colonialism in Ousmane Sembene's Emitai," *CLA Journal*, 24, no. 3 (March 1981), 336–46.

African myths and traditions against the colonial French military's requisition of their rice at the rate of sixty pounds of rice per person. The villagers' final action is spearheaded by its women, who vigorously protest the increasing demands of the French colonial power who seek men and foodstuffs in their overseas colonies to help sustain France's war efforts in Europe.

Emitai is less accessible to world audiences than *Mandabi* because Sembene gives his film a sociohistorical, religious, and political dimension which is inherently Senegalese. He builds his plot on a succession of true events linked to the Senegalese resistance to French colonialism during World War II. His characters, the Diola, live in the small isolated villages of Casamance. They have a long history of resistance to foreign influence and are a good example of traditional African values. Intending to make *Emitai* "a school of history," Sembene connects the Diola's rebellion to a much more distant past than the period illustrated in the film—pointing out the frequency of such occurrences in Africa during the colonial era.[3]

In *Emitai*, Sembene also wanted to represent the mysticism of the Diola and the intimate rapport they entertain with their gods. The Diola's religious convictions encompass a complicated cosmology.[4] They believe in a creator or supreme being and in spirits governing nature. For them, people have a privileged place in the universe and they are in permanent contact with visible and invisible forces. The spirits are intermediaries between the Diola and their gods. They occasionally materialize in human form and hold discussions with the people about the community's vital issues such as the election of a chief. If wars, sickness, or drought disrupt the balance of the universe, the priest will offer sacrifices to the spirits to reconcile the life forces that will, for instance, bring rain and fertility to the fields. Thus, the title of the film is twofold. *Emitai* means "god of thunder," the thunder which brings rain, but it also symbolizes anger and strength. The physical world of *Emitai* from which the Diola's faith emerged is aptly depicted by Sembene in his many shots of the forest where he devotes much attention to the huge and barren baobabs in which people hide, watch, and give signals. Here, the sacred tree is most significant. Old men sit at its foot for their palavers. They pour the blood of sacrificial roosters and goats on its dead trunk in their effort to appease the spirits but also to metaphorically rejuvenate their own manhood. At the same time, they invigorate the collective body of the village, which has been weakened by the scattering and spilling of its young blood abroad. Here one sees that Sembene never draws his characters out of their environment but makes it an indispensable and immediate constituent of his plot. The Diola also believe in reincarnation, but when someone dies this person has to be buried immediately because, without proper funerals, souls will be restless and become wandering spirits who may seek revenge. In reference to the film, it is significant to stress that the priest frequently assumes the function of the chief, thus assuring the political as well as the religious cohesion of the group.

It is, therefore, by design that Ousmane Sembene selected the Diola among the various ethnic groups of Senegal. The Diola have a more egalitarian political system than the other groups. Their independence is legendary (up to the twentieth century), and their religion goes back to ancestral African beliefs untouched by imported religions such as Islam or Christianity. By tradition, they are opposed to the selling of rice and the contents of their granaries are closely kept, which helps explain the villagers' resistance in the film. This resistance is also due to the fact that the amount of rice requested by the French will obviously dangerously deplete the village's rice supply. For them, rice cultivation ensures domestic organization, the division of tasks and the legislative system. Divorces, for instance, can take place only after the rice is harvested so as not to endanger the means of sustenance.

In *Emitai*, African myths and traditions come up against colonialism, and it is the clash between those two antithetic forces and the unevenness of their weapons which brings about the final holocaust of the film. Here, Senegal is under French rule, which began in 1854, following several centuries of Portuguese and English domination since the mid-fifteenth century. One of the Diola villagers even deplores the fact of still being caught between three kinds of colonialism: French (in Casamance), English (in The Gambia, north of Casamance), and Portuguese (in Guinea-Bissau, south of Casamance).

Unlike British colonialism, which was basically anti-assimilationist with its system of indirect rule through existing indigenous institutions, French colonialism pursued a policy of direct rule and theoretical political assimilation. France's *mission civilisatrice* was to convert "barbarians" into French subjects. This implied a total dismissal of centuries of African culture as primitive customs or superstitious beliefs. Consequently, the power of traditional chiefs was diminished by the French administration as they were often treated as low-ranking officials. They were deposed and replaced when they refused to cooperate. This last characteristic lends even more significance to the village chief's rebellion against French authority in *Emitai*.

In addition to its missionaries and administrators, France maintained control over foreign dependencies through the colonial army. The hierarchical pattern of the army generally included white officers, black and white non-commissioned officers, and black privates. The last-named group came from all countries of Western Africa. They were called *tirailleurs* and were in fact black mercenaries sometimes recruited by force, receiving minimal instruction, small salaries, and rifles with which to fight in European wars or put an end to occasional revolts in Africa.[5] In this way, blacks—whether chiefs, civil servants, or soldiers—were used against other blacks to strengthen white rule in French Africa.

Sembene's setting from 1941 to 1944 is not accidental and reflects his interest for crisis situations often found during periods of transition. It throws light upon the new aspect French colonialism had taken in West Africa and particularly in Senegal. At that time, under the Vichy government who had signed an armistice with Germany in 1940, Senegal was subjected to heavy economic exploitation and her representative institutions had been suppressed. Due to influence of Nazi ideology within Pétain's government, the concept of racial superiority was more than ever officially applied to the detriment of the Africans. The recruitment of forced labor among Africans was intensified as was the drafting of men into the armed forces. Farmers were assigned production quotas for exportable foodstuffs. Later, such policies of political, economic, and social discrimination were, at first, hardly altered by the allegiance of West African governors to De Gaulle in 1942. It was only later, in 1944, at the Conference of Brazzaville that a new and more liberal French colonial policy was to be adopted. This conference, under the chairmanship of General De Gaulle, set a basis for the total integration of the colonies into the French community. Yet this concept did not materialize until 1958 at the eve of the independence of all of France's African territories.

In this Second World War context, the black man was socially and psychologically weakened since he was prevented from determining his own destiny and identity as an African. If he refused to cooperate, he was often a dead man; if he surrendered, he degraded himself and was no longer a man. In the village depicted in *Emitai*, the young Diola men have been drafted by force and only the women are left to face the elders' slow and staggering action. They have to take an active role and they become the catalyst of resistance although, or perhaps because, they do not participate in the men's palavers in the sacred wood. It is to be observed that throughout the film, those women are visually represented as a cohesive entity. Although they are individually depicted in their domestic and agricultural tasks or making representative gestures, no repeated performance or other given characteristic allows the viewer to detect personal attributes. This collectiveness is emphasized by the fact that they are continuously referred to as "the women" by the village's men, who are more individualized through their status and social function. In *Emitai*, the common strength and determination of those Casamance women are revealed through long scenes in which they remain silent while being forced to sit in a scorching sun until they disclose where the rice is hidden.

Ousmane Sembene, as in many of his other literary and cinematographic works, breaks with the stereotyped image of the passive and submissive African woman. To understand the role of the woman in *Emitai*, we have to keep in mind that rice has a religious meaning for the Diola since it is offered to the spirits. The woman, therefore, protects the rice because of its religious implications but also because it is she who is responsible for the vital sustenance of the village. In Senegal, except for ploughing, rice is a woman's crop, while peanuts are mainly cultivated by men. So, among the Diola, since the woman takes a substantial part in agricultural tasks she also enjoys more social prerogatives than her counterpart in northern Senegal. This factor was assuredly appealing to Sembene as he wrote his script because he is a firm believer in the equal status of men and women in society. The woman's fecundity is also embodied in the rice and milk she produces. She resists in order to maintain tradition as well as her own social status. The plot of *Emitai* is based on true facts and, in this film, the Senegalese director wishes to illustrate how the African woman has often played an important role in movements of resistance throughout history.[6]

In this struggle between the spiritual and the material, the spear can scarcely oppose the rifle. Traditions are overcome by France's economic needs and modern technology. Sembene takes great care in delineating the fact that the relations between the oppressor and the oppressed are based on economic factors. The villagers' ultimate action is desperate and the imbalance of power somewhat reminds us of Ethiopian peasants throwing spears to the Italian planes invading Ethiopia just before World War II. The unevenness of the forces which are present is dramatically stressed in the last scene of the film where the men, upon hearing the women's voices, put down the baskets of rice and refuse to resume their walk. They are ruthlessly executed on the spot by the African soldiers who open fire under the French lieutenant's command.

In *Emitai*, the filmmaker reacts against the image of the good, irresponsible, simple, childlike, and docile African "savage" which has been diffused by the Western world. In representing Diola myths and traditions, he reacts against the fact that they have long been ignored. But he also fights clichés according to which Africans spontaneously offered themselves on the altar of Europe's battlefields, ever ready to "die magnificently."[7] In the film, one of Sembene's characters says: "First the white man wanted our men and now he wants our rice," while another adds: "This war is not ours, it is the white man's war." Both equally perceive their exploitation.

Also exploited are the tirailleurs, who are made to feel superior to other blacks. In this case, Sembene deals with a theme with which he is very familiar since he served in the French colonial army. He emphasizes the failure of French assimilation policies through a scene in which black soldiers speak broken French like uprooted cultural bastards who are not French and no longer truly African.[8]

In its illustration of French colonialism, *Emitai* stresses the contradictions and the opportunistic aspect of such a system. If colonialism officially debased or negated African myths and traditions, it utilized them as well when opportune: the white commander is aware of the Diola's burial customs and, in preventing the chief's funeral, he uses this element as a way of inducing the villagers' submission.

Finally, it is noteworthy to realize that Ousmane Sembene not only denounces colonialism and its fascist methods of fighting fascism, but also criticizes traditional African religions. For him, "all religions are opiates," in that they provide a spiritual escape from reality.[9] In *Emitai*, the elders lament near the sacred tree: "Where are our gods?" "Where were our gods when the whites raided our village? Where were our gods? Where are they now?" The elders seek shelter in religion to justify their resignation and failure in front of aggression. But before dying, the chief has a dialogue with the spirits.

The spirits: If you have offended the gods, if you no longer believe in us, you will die.
The chief: So I must die, but you will die with me too.

If the chief's words call for the spirits' death, Sembene's current atheistic and socially committed ideology implies that men and women will have to forge their own destiny without relying on supernatural powers.

NOTES

1. From a lecture delivered by Ousmane Sembene at Howard University, Washington, D.C., 21 March 1975.
2. At the beginning of *Emitai*, the following words appear on the screen: "I dedicate this film to all the militants of the African cause."

3. Harold Weaver, "Interview with Ousmane Sembene," *Issue*, vol. 2, n. 4 (1972), p. 58.

4. Louis Vincent Thomas, *Les Diolas* (Dakar: IFAN, 1959).

5. The tirailleurs were soldiers of the regiment of Senegalese troops created in 1857 by Louis Faidherbe, who conquered Senegal.

6. Harold Weaver, "Interview with Ousmane Sembene," p. 58.

7. In Alphonse Sèche, *Les Noirs* (Paris: Payot, 1919), p. 22. Although the book was written after World War I, its themes persisted throughout World War II and thereafter.

8. For adequate realism, Ousmane Sembene includes three languages in his film: Diola, French, and pidgin French.

9. Sembene's lecture, Howard University, 1975.

8
XALA (1974): REALISM AND SYMBOLISM

> The national middle class which takes over power at the end of the colonial regime is an underdeveloped middle class. It has practically no economic power, and in any case it is in no way commensurate with the bourgeoisie of the mother country it hopes to replace.[1]

Xala, whose Wolof title means "impotence," is a perfect illustration of this quote from Frantz Fanon, the well-known Martiniquan psychiatrist and political writer. It is the only film of Sembene's which centers primarily on Senegal's new middle class. This two-hour color motion picture shot in both French and Wolof is a parable about the sexual and social impotence of El Hadji Abdoukader Beye. El Hadji is a Muslim title granted men who have participated in the pilgrimage to Mecca, Prophet Mohammed's birthplace. El Hadji is a seemingly prosperous polygamous middle-aged importer-exporter recently elected to the Senegalese Chamber of Commerce. On his wedding night, he finds out that he is unable to perform his sexual duties with his third wife. His marabouts confirm that a curse has been made against him. As he relentlessly seeks cure for his im-

Chapter adapted from Françoise Pfaff, "Three Faces of Africa: Women in Xala," *Jump Cut*, n. 27 (1982), pp. 27–31.

potence, he neglects his business. Soon, prior embezzlements are discovered and El Hadji ends up in social disgrace. His only hope of regaining his manhood lies in a beggar's alleged ability to remove the curse. The beggar placed the curse on El Hadji as revenge for his past misappropriation of his land.

The very first sequences of *Xala* indicate that El Hadji personifies the ideological, political, and social concerns of Senegal's mercantile elite fifteen years after independence. Indeed, the wealth of El Hadji is fragile; it is that of the national bourgeoisie, whose apparent power relies on its ability to trade with former colonial "metropoles," whose dictates they have to endure. Fanon contemptuously acknowledges the shallowness of this bourgeoisie by writing:

> From the beginning the national bourgeoisie directs its efforts toward activities of the intermediary type. The basis of its strength is found in its aptitude for trade and small business enterprises, and in securing commissions. It is not its money that works, but its business acumen. It does not go in for investments and it cannot achieve that accumulation of capital necessary to the birth and blossoming of an authentic bourgeoisie.[2]

The title and the content of Sembene's film (as well as his novel of the same name from which it is adapted) places emphasis on male genitalia. Still, El Hadji's impotence reflects as well that of the Senegalese nation, culturally, politically, and socially emasculated by its colonial inheritance and present dependence. *Xala*'s satirical mood is conveyed through the close-ups of faces and situations in a succession of sequences depicting an emerging African middle class who apparently hides its lack of economic power under the cloak of prestige expenses, while their country is faced with a multitude of predicaments.

It is through the women with whom he is related that El Hadji's power is shown and, in turn, negated. Yet in *Xala*, the female characters are much more than mere appendages to the principal character. They become an intrinsic part of his social ascent and subsequent decline. They function on both a sociorealistic and symbolic level and can be viewed as integral characters whose structural and ideological facets not only mirror but are equal in importance to that of the male protagonist.

Awa, El Hadji's oldest wife, appears as the embodiment of African traditions even if her environment is no longer purely traditional. She lives in a house located in an affluent Dakar neighborhood with her own children and servants. Like El Hadji, she is in her late forties or early fifties. Tall, with a slow and dignified gait, she reveals no emotion in her ebony mask. She apparently accepts silently her preordained role as a wife within an African polygamous marital situation. Her seemingly relentless abnegation and distant behavior do not always match her inner feelings. She goes to her husband's third wedding. If she divorces him as her daughter Rama suggests, she will lose the privileges conferred on a first wife by Islam. She tells Rama: "You think I'd find a husband. I'll be a third or fourth wife." Awa depends socially and economically on El Hadji. She compromises for emotional security and financial support by reluctantly submitting to the female sex-role expectations in her patriarchal Islamic society. Awa's obedience is expected from her community. When her son asks her why she should go to witness her husband's wedding, she answers with resignation: "Unfortunately, I have to go. What would people say?"

Although the rules of a polygamous society shape her conduct, Awa in turn uses these rules to assert her authority over Oumi, El Hadji's second wife. When El Hadji asks Awa to come with him inside Oumi's house, Awa refuses in the name of the marital laws that force her into submission. It is through them that El Hadji's first wife confronts the husband she must otherwise obey. She points out: "Do you forget I'm your first? Go and say hello for me." Later, when Awa sits with Oumi in the reception room, Awa calms her co-wife's verbalized frustration with an ironic statement which stresses their forced solidarity. Awa advocates patience since she understands Oumi's feelings against N'Goné, the third wife, because Awa had undoubtedly experienced them herself in regard to Oumi. She tells Oumi with a bitter humor: "Patience does not kill. If so, I would be dead." When Awa leaves the ceremony she expresses some kinship and understanding as she invites El Hadji's second wife to her house: "Do come by and see me sometimes. Don't forget I'm your elder."

In *Xala*, the contrast between Awa and El Hadji's second wife, Oumi, is seen strikingly during a scene of the third wedding where the two women sit together, outcasts because of El Hadji's new pride and happiness. Wearing a traditional African dress, Awa shows the resignation of a patient village woman. Oumi, who wears a modish wig and a European dress with a voluptuous revealing neckline, refrains with great difficulty from expressing her rage and discomfort at being a participant at her husband's third wedding. Her youth and sophistication might have led her to believe that she had a greater chance of ensuring forever El Hadji's preference. Assured of her sexual appeal, she pitilessly reminds El Hadji (then sexually impotent) of his duties towards her: "It is my turn. I want you at the house tonight. You know I am always ready." Oumi arrogantly stands up to El Hadji, implying that she would recognize her husband's authority only as long as he also fulfills his sex role. Financially much greedier than Awa (she asks El Hadji for money on the day of the wedding), Oumi remains with her husband until she witnesses the first signs of his downfall. At that point she leaves him. She departs with a truck loaded with the goods and the furniture given to her in El Hadji's wealthier days. If Awa embodies a reassuring, stabilized, pure motherliness completely divested of apparent sexuality, Oumi appears as the seductive and destructive temptress—an archetype usually connected by male authors to man's misery. Oumi leaves El Hadji when he is no longer able to satisfy her sexual demands and economic security.

N'Goné, El Hadji's third wife, only retains Sembene's attention because she illustrates El Hadji's status-seeking greed. In *Xala*, a long panoramic shot of the endless parade of the gifts displayed by El Hadji as her dowry stresses the corrupted patterns of such a tradition.[3] N'Goné is merely traded and exhibited to El Hadji's middle-aged friends and colleagues. The film offers a mordant comment on El Hadji's "economics of marriage." El Hadji, rather grossly, praises his "purchase" to the president of the Chamber of Commerce by stressing

N'Goné's "virginal value" as well as that of his other wives when he married them. He tells him: "My first wife was a virgin and so was my second." Here, virginity reflects a property received intact, thus ensuring the groom's prestige. N'Goné's mother acknowledges the groom's prerogatives as the mother provides the daughter with some last words concerning the daughter's duties as a subservient wife, who should only aspire to please her husband. The mother stresses: "Man is the master, you must always be available. Don't raise your voice. Be submissive." Through N'Goné, El Hadji intends to exhibit his social dominance as well as his immediate virility. N'Goné's role in the film and for El Hadji is little more than a *femme objet*. This is illustrated on the poster made for the film in which the middle third of her naked back lies in the foreground while the beggar dispossessed by El Hadji stands in a reduced scale in the background. El Hadji himself is seen from the back, departing with his attaché case. This poster directly presents graphic correlation between the businessman's sexual and economic impotence. In the film, El Hadji is preparing for intercourse, N'Goné's naked back is shown in the same position as on the poster, lying motionless on the nuptial bed. At that point, the camera swiftly switches from the indifferent body of the *grande horizontale* to her picture hanging on the wall, frozen in the distance as if out of El Hadji's physical reach. N'Goné's photograph seems to be used to emphasize a haunting positive/negative picture of her desirable self whom El Hadji is unable to deflower and "possess." Then, like Oumi, N'Goné disassociates herself from El Hadji in his decline since the main purpose of her union with him was financial support for herself and her family.

At this point, it might be interesting to see how Sembene himself sees El Hadji's wives as closely related to the various stages of the male character's life. "He married his first wife before he became somebody. Having improved his economic and social status, he takes a second wife, who, so to speak, parallels the second historical stage of his life. His third wife, who is his daughter's age but without her mentality, is only there for self-satisfaction."[4] Here it is important to keep in mind the parallel Sembene draws between the first two wives and the two historical stages of El Hadji's life. Later, the same analogy will be set between those two wives and the historical evolution of Senegal.

The other important woman in *Xala* is Rama, El Hadji's daughter by his first wife. Rama is as aggressive and assertive as N'Goné is passive and submissive. She is as articulate in her speech pattern as N'Goné is silent. As an unmarried student with intellectual potential and as a young militant for Africanization, Rama often defies her father by speaking Wolof, knowing that he prefers to use French. On the day of the wedding, Rama confronts El Hadji by telling him: "Every polygamous man is a liar." This interaction between father and daughter ends abruptly with him slapping her face. Rama's rebellion is especially meaningful since, according to the African tradition, children are not to confront their elders and girls even less than boys. Awa is shocked by her daughter's audacity. Puzzled, El Hadji asks her one day in his office: "Why do you answer in Wolof when I talk to you in French? Do you need anything?" El Hadji reaches for his wallet trying to bridge the gap between them with money. Rama tells him that she does not have any financial needs and that she is only concerned about her mother whom he neglects. She refuses to drink bottled French mineral water, which her father drinks and also uses to fill the radiator of his Mercedes. Since she is more opposed to what such French mineral water represents than to the extravagance of its expensive use, her refusal and implicit preference for local spring water has a key political significance.

Rama stands tall in her father's office as she resists El Hadji. Dressed in the traditional Senegalese boubou, Rama wears a short Afro hair style instead of traditional Senegalese braids. For transportation, she rides a moped. This associates her somewhat androgynous appearance with the winged swiftness and freedom of a modern-day Amazon.[5] Rama is not attracted by the luxurious automotive machines of the Western world. She only uses the aspects of Western culture that can serve in daily life—education, modern technology—and does not confer on imported goods the same fetishistic quality as her father. In spite of the concise development of her character, Rama's function in the film is trenchant. Sembene visually stresses her independence of mind as well as her freedom as a character by presenting her alone in many more shots than the other female characters. She is not relegated to a stereotyped role as are Oumi and N'Goné.

In *Xala*, Sembene has schematized his female protagonists. They become archetypical and have a role to play in Sembene's sociopolitical dialectics. Awa, Oumi, and Rama are more significant than N'Goné, who is nothing more than the most recent status symbol acquired by El Hadji—although we are not to forget that it is she who indirectly triggers his downfall. The three women are metaphors for Africa. Although these three characters are to be perceived as types, they do not represent all Senegalese women, most of whom still live in rural areas. On a symbolic level, these three female characters are equated with Africa at different periods of its evolution. But geographic limitations in the analogy are neglected, just as the urban Senegalese El Hadji becomes a symbolic embodiment of the African nouveaux riches.

To deal with women characters as metaphors, thus transferring some of their qualities to something other than themselves, appears hazardous. In many instances, this process might simplify and thus divest the character of human attributes. It might also reduce or disassociate the object from the symbol for which it stands. As an artist, Sembene's merit lies in his ability to go beyond a mere imitation of life, beyond his characters' reality, without stultifying or neglecting an important part of such realities. One of Sembene's highest achievements is the successful transposition of his women characters' qualities to the symbolic realm, within which his overall political message acquires increased significance.

The women in *Xala* live within the confines of a modern urban polygamous family. In contrast, Islam in earlier years had flourished within a traditional African rural context, and it was a religion readily accepted by the Senegalese who had already adopted polygamous social patterns within their agricultural society: the more wives, the more hands to cultivate the fields and ensure the sustenance of the compounds. In such a situation, older wives often welcome younger wives to participate in their domestic and agricultural tasks. Many women recognize the benefit of having additional help in running their households. In such instances, co-wives are useful in times of illness and other incapacitation in rural areas. In *Xala*, El Hadji's wealth has separated the co-wives into different dwellings in an urban environment. For him, the more wives, the more prestige and status. The family unit has lost its closeness, and the co-wives envy each other although they hardly know each other. This situation already present in rural polygamous families, is exaggerated in an urban context. Such a geographic scattering of El Hadji's wives not only adds to his expenses, stress, and dilemma, but it also reduces his authority as a patriarchal figure. His separate houses create new social units headed chiefly by wives. The father and theoretical master of the household is only episodically present. El Hadji's family lives on the fringe of two worlds: Africa and the West. El Hadji himself reflects this hybrid. His amulets, Muslim faith, and Mercedes, in turn, represent pre-Islamic Africa, Islamic Africa, and Westernized Africa.

Oumi is attracted by the mirages of the Western consumer society. As expected, Sembene shows a limited interest in this character who, although partially Westernized, is still part of traditional Africa by her situation within a polygamous marriage. In the film, she is merely a caricature. Sembene distrusts her because of her cupidity and her shallowness. She occasionally provides comic relief through the film's satirical description of how she affects an excessive Western mannerism. In her eagerness to copy Western mores, she fits the traits of the "get-rich-quick middle class" which "becomes not even the replica of Europe, but its caricature."[6]

Awa (in Wolof her name refers to the original woman called Eve in the Judeo-Christian world without Eve's temptress connotations), although in a transitional world, mostly represents Africa in its essence. Awa is Eve, the giver of life, but even more so she is a model for Senegalese womankind. She personifies the dignity, reserve, patience, and loyalty often attributed by African authors to the traditional African woman. Some of her qualities are described by author Sarah Kala. "African traditional civilization was an agricultural one. . . .

The African woman used to be a strong economic asset and neither polygamy nor the bride price must be regarded as degrading factors. . . . The African woman was an advisor whenever a crisis arose. She was in charge of the education of her children, her daughters especially, and was a complement to her husband."[7]

Awa is the wife El Hadji addresses mostly in Wolof. At home, he recovers his "Africanness." He goes to her after having been deserted by his two other wives. We also expect that it is in her company that he will end his life. Sembene emphasizes Awa's characteristics by contrasting them to those of Rama, who is very attached to her mother. By assigning Rama this trait, Sembene refers to the traditional "cult of the mother," which goes back to matriarchal pre-Islamic African societies. Rama wishes to liberate her mother from her polygamous bonds and suggests that Awa divorces, an act which still brands women as outcasts in modern-day Senegal, where a woman is socially defined by her husband. Rama is close to her mother, who appears as a custodian of traditional African values. Yet Rama is ready to reject traditional values, which she thinks will hamper the development of Senegal as a modern nation. Her use of Wolof seems a way to recover African identity, as does her refusal to drink the mineral water imported from France, thus showing her opposition to Senegal's economic and cultural dependence on France. One thinks about Fanon, who saw in the establishment of the French language a means used by France to ensure its influence in its former empire. Rama rejects a world expressed and interpreted through the use of French. She refuses, as Sartre would say, "the alienation which a foreign intellect imposes . . . under the name of assimilation."[8] She also could serve as an illustration of another quotation from Sartre: "It is thus for the black to die of the white world to be reborn of the black soul, as the platonic philosopher dies of the body to be reborn of the truth."[9]

Obviously, Rama's disagreement with her father goes beyond the usual generation gap. When they try to communicate, they each use a language they assume ideologically so that language then loses part of its function since it does not allow a true dialogue. When El Hadji, the businessman, tries to set their exchange on financial grounds, he increases their disagreement. Sembene explains this clash between father and daughter:

In *Xala*, this elderly man who might have talked about Senegalese independence no longer agrees with his daughter. His daughter implicitly argues with him about a national language. At this point he has lost his authority. There is, however, something which lies behind these problems. *Xala* takes place in a period of transition. In all periods of transition there is always an opposition to the father because fathers have always a tendency to be conservative.[10]

Rama is a positive and refreshing counterpart to her father, who represents the corrupted bourgeoisie that robs the masses and perpetuates the French neo-colonial presence in Africa. She confronts her father and, contrary to her bitterly resigned mother, she vehemently protests against El Hadji's new marriage and polygamy in general. Unattached and single, she is the only woman in *Xala* who does not have to grant sexual favors for economic support from a man. Although she depends financially on her father, this confers a certain degree of autonomy to Rama as a character and accounts for her outspokenness. The divorce she advocates works on two levels: it is her mother's as well as Senegal's divorce from a paternalistic neo-colonial rule. Rama is hope, hope for the future when Senegal will be ruled by leaders able to keep the positive aspects of traditional Africa while making good use of Western technology. She is the only character in *Xala* who has succeeded in assimilating both traditional African and European cultures into a coherent symbiosis. She embodies Sembene's wishes for a modern and truly independent Africa. According to him, "this young girl is like a step forward in a society which must find a synthesis. It must do so, but how? One can no longer be traditional but neither can one completely resign oneself to European ways."[11]

Except in very rare instances, Sembene's works both in print and in film have an abundance of strong and meaningful women opposed to weak and/or shallow men. Although brought up as a Muslim, Sembene spent almost half of his life outside a strictly Muslim context. And, as a humanist desiring to reshape Africa, he breaks with the accepted norm of a male-dominated society. To account for the strength of Sembene's female characters, one has to refer to the Senegalese environment upon which they were patterned. There, in colonial and neo-colonial times, it is men more so than women who, through education and business, have always had most contacts with the West. Sembene visualizes the men's consequential assimilation as a loss of self (to which El Hadji's "xala" also refers). Sembene contends that traditionally African women, as life sources and links between generations, have been the custodians and the transmitters of African authenticity. From such a perspective, the writer/filmmaker has aptly chosen heroines as metaphors for Africa. In so doing, he wants to re-endow their fictional portrayal with the strong features which have always been related to their role in the Senegalese society.

Sembene's interest in the African woman as a symbol also utilizes the image of women's fecundity. Transmitter of the past, the African woman bears children and as such becomes the custodian of the future. Rama, Awa's daughter, serves as a metaphor for a future Africa, united and powerful, having erased the boundaries imposed by nineteenth-century Western colonialism. Sembene's own Pan-African ideals seem reflected in a shot of Rama as she argues with El Hadji in his office. Two maps are hanging in this room. A medium shot shows El Hadji sitting at his desk in front of a political map of Africa that depicts its present frontiers (this same kind of map is also found at the Chamber of Commerce). Rama is standing. She wears a Senegalese boubou whose purple stripes match a purple map of Africa shown behind her, one with no national boundaries. Here, the camera, with its power to fix and emphasize objects, supplies the spectator with a symbolic image of Rama/Sembene's ideology. This representation becomes a crucial element in the filmmaker's dialectic narrative based on African women as metaphors. Also, a brief shot of posters representing Cabral and Samori in Rama's bedroom visually reinforces our sense of her progressive ideas.[12] In *Xala*, the picture of Cabral, the socialist African leader, in conjunction with that of Samori, the fighter against French colonialism, reflect the continuity of the African determination towards freedom. Sembene presents a message not only expanded through time but also through space, since Samori was from Mali and Cabral from Guinea-Bissau. Rama personifies the new African woman who, jointly with the African man, will actively participate in the progress of Africa. And, Sembene thinks (as did Marx concerning women in Western societies) that the degree of emancipation of African women is the mirror and the measure of the general emancipation of Africa from its colonial and neo-colonial fetters. He observes that "Africa can't develop without the participation of her women. . . . We are still searching for our destiny as Africans. Yet in the society we are going to build, women will play an important role."[13]

Not only must the African woman participate in the struggle for a new Africa, but Sembene implies that Africa, in order to grow and truly assert itself, should be fecund and nurturing like a woman. In Africa, more than anywhere else, the woman is seen as the link between generations, for she has the privilege of reproduction (her cycles of fecundity parallel those of the earth). Here, a reference should be made in respect to the part played by matriarchal African societies in which matrilineage ensured the social and cultural continuity of given communities whose law and custom centered on the mother. Some African religions assert the presence of female water goddesses, from whom life proceeds (there is officially no goddess in the Jewish or Christian religion, although the worship some Catholics exhibit towards Mary, mother of God, might indeed place her at the rank of a quasi goddess), and this is additional evidence of the vital use of women as a metaphor in African cultures. Sembene, who is a product of these cultures, intimates that the African woman is earth/land and "Mother Africa" the genitrix of a new Africa. A woman is fertile like soil and soil is fertile like a woman. Africa is fecund like a woman. Furthermore, El Hadji is impotent (inability to "plough" through the "earth"/penetrate the woman) because he has misused the fecundity of Africa/woman to assert his social and male ascendancy. A true example of the "rapacious bourgeoisie" denounced by Fanon,[14] El Hadji first robbed a peasant (the beggar) of his land and then diverted tons of rice (another fertility symbol) to his own profit. Africa and N'Goné are fecund but El Hadji is unable to impregnate them because of his socioeconomical/sexual impotence, thus causing the barrenness/sterility of Africa/woman. This sexual metaphor represents the crux of Sembene's political message as conveyed through *Xala*.

In *Xala*, Awa, Oumi, and Rama are viewed as the symbolic types for a pedagogic demonstration since they feature Africa at various stages of its development. Sembene denounces Oumi by ridiculing her, not because of who she is (an African woman of limited schooling who became El Hadji's second wife) but because of her metaphoric hybrid nature. The writer-filmmaker favors Awa and Rama. Rama's kinship is not adventitious. Literally and figuratively Rama emerged from Awa's womb. Their link is as strong as the bond existing in ancient Africa when the magical secrets of curing were passed from mother to daughter. Transitional Africa featured through Oumi has to "pack up" literally and metaphorically (as it happens in the film) her Western material goods and disappear with them since she has distorted them by overrating them. Awa and Rama both remain with the humiliated El Hadji. Awa cries at the sight of her husband's humiliation, and Rama condescends to speak French to a policeman to protect the beggars and thus help her father who depends on the beggars' goodwill to regain his virility. The final freeze frame suggests that both Awa and Rama will share his future life.

In the last scene of *Xala*, the impotent African man is surrounded by both the traditional (Awa) and the modern politically committed African woman (Rama) as he expects to recover his virility. This is to be achieved through the purifying spitting of the beggars. Their spitting has a spiritual, moral, and physical regenerative function—a rite of passage from one state of being to another. In many African countries, such rituals are connected with simultaneous death and rebirth. The life transitions they represent are met ceremonially and involve magic. It is in such a frame of reference that one has to view the beggars' magical ability to remove the spell they put on El Hadji so that he may be able to regain his manhood. Significantly, it was the beggars' leader who had been dispossessed as a result of El Hadji's misuse of earth/woman. Women beggars are absent in this spitting ritual. The male beggars who institute El Hadji's sexual rebirth have an appearance— in rags, blind, with one arm, one leg, or no legs—that could also ironically refer to both physical and social amputation. The metaphoric impact of such a dispossessed brotherhood would certainly have been lessened had women been included among the beggars. Their absence should by no means be attributed to a biased choice on Sembene's part but rather to a symbolic continuum: the curse of male impotence as it is put and removed by the same male, the blind leader of the beggars. Sembene's choice was also probably made for the sake of verisimilitude. In present day Senegal, female beggars are mostly seen in the streets of downtown Dakar with young children, even babies. It would be too conspicuous and too risky, with possible scuffles with the police and even imprisonment, to allow women with children to march to Awa's house in an affluent Dakar neighborhood.

As El Hadji endures the beggars' ritual trial, he is grotesquely crowned by one of the beggars with a white orange-flower crown (formerly worn by N'Goné as a part of her wedding attire), a reminder of the virginity of the woman he was not able to deflower/possess. At this time, two oppressed segments of the Senegalese society have much in common. As a minority within a male-dominated Islamic society, women's status parallels that of the deprived Senegalese masses repressed by the same patriarchal bourgeoisie. The filmmaker's final images imply that the two groups' emancipation is joined and interrelated. In *Xala*, portraying Awa, Oumi, and Rama, Sembene implicitly condemns female subservience and polygamy. Through El Hadji's impotence and downfall, he suggests that black Africa's middle class is doomed to lose its power unless it stops aping the Western world in a state of complacent cultural and economic dependency and identifies with the social needs and aspirations of all Africans.

NOTES

1. Frantz Fanon, *The Wretched of the Earth* (New York: Grove Press, 1979), p. 149. This book was first published by François Maspero (Paris, 1961) under the title *Les Damnés de la Terre*.

2. Frantz Fanon, *The Wretched of the Earth*, p. 179.

3. Many Africans, among them female Senegalese writer and journalist Annette M'Baye, state that dowry (cattle, food, materials) used to be a proof of the seriousness of the groom's intention. He was offering gifts to his wife's family as a token of his good intentions and ability to support a spouse. It is usually believed that Western capitalism and colonialism distorted the primary function of such dowry by placing emphasis on the trade pattern in which the wife was merely "purchased" in exchange for material goods.

4. Noureddine Ghali, "Ousmane Sembene," *Cinéma 76*, n. 208 (1976), p. 88. Author's translation.

5. Here, the term "modern-day Amazon" suggests that Rama is related to both modernism and African traditionalism. Aicha N'Doye writes about the Amazons of African history: "The famous Amazons of the King of Dahomey are witnesses of the part played by the females in war and fights." See Aicha N'Doye, contributor, *La Civilisation de la Femme dans la Tradition Africaine*, (Paris: Présence Africaine, 1975), p. 275.

6. Frantz Fanon, *The Wretched of the Earth*, p. 175.

7. Sarah Kala, contributor, *La Civilisation de la Femme dans la Tradition Africaine*, p. 92.

8. Jean-Paul Sartre, *Black Orpheus* (Paris: Présence Africaine, 1976), pp. 30–31.

9. Ibid., p. 31.

10. From a series of interviews with Ousmane Sembene conducted by the author in Senegal in 1978.

11. Jean and Ginette Delmas, "Ousmane Sembene: Un Film est un Débat," *Jeune Cinéma*, n. 99 (December 1976–January 1977), p. 16. Author's translation.

12. Amilcar Cabral, although killed before the independence of Guinea-Bissau, is considered one of the nation's main liberators from Portuguese rule. Samori Touré was for a time the architect of a resurrected Mali empire who opposed French colonialism in Africa at the end of the nineteenth century. Captured in 1898, he died in 1900 in exile in Gabon.

13. Sembene to author, Senegal, 1978.

14. Frantz Fanon, *The Wretched of the Earth*, p. 168.

9
CEDDO (1976): A STORY OF THE PAST WITH CONTEMPORARY SIGNIFICANCE

In *Ceddo*, Sembene's latest film to date, Senegalese history is once more scrutinized and revalued because, according to him "our history was not taught to people of my generation. We know the dates, the legends, but we don't clearly see what happened. Our aim here is to dramatize history and to teach it so as not to let others teach it to us."[1]

Ceddo is a condensed representation of the various forces present in a small village north of Dakar at the time of the slave trade: traditional African rule, European mercantilism, Muslim and Christian expansion. It opens with the capture of the king's daughter by an insubordinate villager, a Ceddo, followed by various attempts to deliver the princess, the mysterious death of the king, the imam's ascension to power, and his subsequent decline and death.

For many Senegalese and others versed in Senegalese history, the title of the film *Ceddo* immediately brings to mind the unyielding spirit of the Ceddo who are not an ethnic group but a people linked by a common thought. For the Wolof, Serer, Soce, and Pular, "to be a Ceddo" is a state of mind. Traditionally, the Ceddo have been the custodians and the defenders of the African identity, initially rebelling against Muslim expansion in Senegal.

At the beginning of the Islamic expansion, the people who hesitated to accept the new religion were called "Ced-do," that is "people from outside," outside the spiritual circles of Mohammed. They were the last holders of African spiritualism before it became tinged with Islam or Christianity. The Ceddo from Pakao resisted the Muslims who wanted to convert them, with a suicidal opposition. Their wives and children drowned themselves in springs in order to remain faithful to their African spirituality.[2]

According to Sembene's printout, distributed when the film was released, *Ceddo* takes place in the course of the seventeenth century when the slave trade started to flourish and when both Islam and Christianity were spreading through West Africa. Although *Ceddo* allegedly takes place in the seventeenth century, its scope goes beyond that era. The insertion of a nineteenth-century African mask, that of a twentieth-century umbrella, and an unexpected flash forward to a huge African Catholic mass of recent years expand the historical perspective of the film, which is a two-hour long account of a two-day story. All the facts which are illustrated in *Ceddo* are authentic and occurred at the same place where the film was shot. For instance, Sembene had a whole village built on location according to historical documents, and he invited a Catholic priest and an imam to supervise the religious rituals shown in the film. Yet, in spite of such concerns for accuracy, Sembene stipulates that the viewer should not try to define the chronologically historical context of the film but rather assess the symbolic value of a plot based on a composite of historical episodes. He explains: "*Ceddo* is a film of reflection, bringing together bits and pieces of facts and authentic events that took place in a period spanning the centuries to the present day."[3]

In its form, *Ceddo* fits cultural patterns which are both African and universal. It is primarily a Senegalese epic which gives preeminence to verbal flourishes, oratorical encounters, and elevated heroic mood. Yet if *Ceddo* is definitely Senegalese in inspiration, it includes characters (king, princess, imam/great wizard, noblemen, and merchants) and situations (the delivery of a beautiful princess, the affront calling for revenge, and the initiatory quest of fearless warriors) which are timelessly ubiquitous and appeal to universal audiences. In most cultures, one finds stories comparable to that of the film and according to which whoever usurps and misuses power should be punished. Then, stylistically, *Ceddo* uses devices frequently found in classic Greek, English, and French theater and in many oral and written narratives worldwide, striving to present archetypical characters and symbolic actions rather than a detailed account of the history on which their plot is based.

Ceddo opens with the introduction of three alien forces at work in a Senegalese village, but, throughout the plot, the filmmaker's attention focuses primarily on Islam. The omnipresence of the imam in this motion picture illustrates the pervading infiltration of Islam both by sword and by politics which had started in Senegal as far back as the ninth century. Many Muslim scholars eventually became part of the kings' court and participated in their councils. This clarifies why Sembene gradually features the imam's greed to expand his spiritual leadership into temporal sovereignty. He equates the imam's aspirations with the present-day political ambitions and influence of the Muslim clergy in Senegal and other countries such as Iran. The cinematographer justifies his personal attack on some Islamic leaders (not the essence of the Islamic faith).

Let me scan quickly over the history of Islam. Islam originated in Mecca within a feudal context. The prophet Mohammed advocated freedom for all slaves. As long as he stayed in Mecca, Mohammed was very progressive and he had a great spiritual and ideological impact. Yet, when Mohammed went into exile, he dethroned a king and took power. How and why did this happen? These are some of the contradictions of Islam. Then, later, Islam was introduced to West Africa by Mohammed's spiritual heirs. From the beginning, they opposed feudalism but their presence, because of their scholarship, was tolerated by the Africans. In Mali, fetishists and Muslims were living together. The mosques were respected and nobody came to desecrate them. However, when the Muslims became more powerful, they decided to suppress all the other religions. They did the same thing in Ghana and Timbuctu. The Gao empire was destroyed by the Muslims. Today, there are African Muslim leaders who are collaborating with foreign imperialism the same way they collaborated with colonialism and slavery. We know that the essence of Islam is not at stake but this should not prevent us from spotting the corrupt leaders of the Islamic faith.[4]

As in the case of *Emitai*, to understand *Ceddo* fully it is necessary to study very closely how French colonialism and Christianity infiltrated West Africa. Thus, it is important to recall that some European powers had already set foot on the coastal regions of the African continent as early as the fifteenth century during the Portuguese exploration of the West Coast of Africa. Soon after, the Dutch, Spaniards, English, and French started to emulate the venture of the Portuguese. In the seventeenth century, attracted by the profit of the slave trade with the New World, these powers increased their efforts in the establishment of new trading posts along the coast as well as along the banks of the principal easily accessible rivers. Soon, in spite of their relatively late coming into Africa, the English and the French were to exert a greater colonial imperialism than the Portuguese.

In *Ceddo*, Sembene investigates the Africans' participation in the slave trade. He rejects the commonplace Manichaeism according to which all of Africa's miseries are solely related to Western slave trade, colonialism, and imperialism. He denies Africans the right to consider themselves perpetually victims of history. He invites them to question those legitimate power structures which permitted and in some cases invited foreign powers to enter the African continent and carry out the relentless exploitation of its human and material resources. With *Ceddo*, Ousmane Sembene sheds light upon the social hierarchy of a caste system which allowed for slaves (prisoners from defeated tribes) to be sold to Western traders. He sustains with some irony: "it is not true that Africa was a marvelous continent before the coming of the Europeans. Yet, it is true that they have, in a way, made things worse. During the colonial era, it was fair enough to attribute all our evils to colonialism because the fundamental contradiction was between colonizers and colonized people."[5]

Sembene believes that now, two decades after most African

countries have become independent, it is time to reject such a dualistic and complacent approach in favor of a more rigorous examination of history. "Africa must start to question itself and see the role played by Africans in the past. Over a five-century time span, we experienced slave trade and colonialism. How did this happen and how did we allow this to happen?"[6]

History also discloses that soon the European traders were "protected" by soldiers and that the efforts of both were geared towards establishing permanent settlements in Senegal. Before long, missionaries joined the settlers. At the time when *Ceddo* takes place, the missionaries were little more than trade post chaplains, either unconcerned with the moral issues of slavery or profiting by it through personally owning or selling slaves. In *Ceddo*, the missionary is Catholic, indicating along with the presence of *fleur-de-lis* branded slaves that the trading post is indeed French. The Catholic priest has only one African disciple and his impact cannot, by any means, be compared to that of the imam. This is historically explained by the fact that Islam had long preceded Christianity in sub-Saharan Africa and that the conversion of Africans to Christianity developed only in the eighteenth and nineteenth centuries.

Another reference to Senegal's past will help to comprehend in Sembene's film the abduction of the king's daughter by a Ceddo who disapproves of the king's political weakness and his vulnerability to foreign expansionism. In effect, as one looks over the time span from the fifteenth to the seventeenth century, one observes that the kingdom of Cayor (in the same region, near Mbour, where Sembene shot his film) did not offer a continuous resistance to foreign influence, whether Muslim or European, because it had been weakened by internal dissensions. Its past, however, abounds in heroic deeds in which both women and *Tyeddo* (another spelling for Ceddo) were actively involved. Cayor was once a part of the Djolof empire from which it seceded in the sixteenth century. From the time of its secession, thirty kings ruled this state. Cayor's social strata consisted of the nobility, free peasants, and slaves. It is to be noted that some slaves (the Tyeddo or royal slaves) had a significant political and military role. Thus, in spite of the fact that the Ceddo were at the bottom of the social ladder, the power of the kings of Cayor often depended on the Ceddo's backing. Hence, the Ceddo who practiced the African animist religion were good allies of their kings in their struggle against Muslim and Christian expansion. Later, in the nineteenth century, a Cayor king by the name of Lat-Dior successfully maintained his rule for twenty-five years, in spite of French interference, because of the Tyeddo. When he converted himself to Islam, he was disapproved of by his Tyeddo soldiers and in the end he was unable to resist French intrusion without their support. Other similar events account for the power of the Ceddo in Senegalese history as well as for their indomitable spirit of resistance against foreign invasion reflected in *Ceddo*.

The initial scenes of *Ceddo*, as is the case in *Emitai*, describe the everyday activities of the village in which the action takes place. A woman with naked breasts follows the custom of morning wash ups with water poured from a calabash. Others spin thread or pound millet into flour. Then, two men go to the trading post where slaves are kept shackled in a hut. The women trade some agricultural products for pieces of European printed cotton. Suddenly, shouts are heard and some women are seen rushing back to the village to announce the princess's abduction.

The princess is kept prisoner by a Ceddo. By such gesture he seeks to alter the king's hesitant ruling and his sympathies towards the teachings of the imam. Princess Dior is about twenty. She wears the traditional Senegalese attire and rich adornments which reflect her noble extraction. She does not fear her young abductor. She is very aware of her social status and arrogantly addresses him in the following terms: "You are a slave, don't you know who I am?" The Ceddo is not affected by her words. He is ready to sacrifice his own life to adhere to his self-imposed mission. He tells a griot: "It is her life or mine." The princess may acknowledge the Ceddo's courage, but her own determination and contempt are reflected in the words she addresses him through the griot: "Fara, tell him the only way I'll leave here is on his back." Far from being intimidated by the princess's provocative threats, he limits with a string the area within which she is to stay, adding: "If you cross this, I'll kill you."

In the village, upon learning his daughter's fate, the king orders a meeting of all his subjects. A drummer announces to the villagers: "The king has called a meeting of the people. Everyone is required to attend. Those who don't will be punished and their possessions will be taken." As the council, to which imam, trader, and missionary are invited, gathers, the griot sings the praises of the converted king whose "reign is the will of Allah." During some vehement verbal exchanges, the Ceddo of the village beseech him to enforce religious freedom. The councilmen appeal to Prince Biram, King Tioub's son, to deliver his sister. Amidst these palavers, Saxewar, to whom the princess is betrothed, comes riding to the village.[7] He assumes as his duty the rescue of his bride to be. He tells the king: "I have accepted the terms of the dowry. . . . I swear that I'll deliver her and marry her." Another prince, Madior, the king's nephew, considers the princess as his legitimate spouse since in this society, before the coming of Islam, matrilineage entitled him to seek the throne. This privilege is thus denied by Biram, the king's son, who bases his denial on the teachings of Islam. He states: "You are my cousin but we are Muslims and Islam forbids matriarchy." Biram's assertion is acknowledged by the imam who expounds: "The son is the rightful heir according to Mohammed." Madior refers to the ancient laws which enthroned his uncle who is now abiding by the laws of Islam. The king's attitude and faithfulness to the patriarchal precepts of Islam is subsequently violently denounced by Madior, who now joins the ranks of his opponents after declaring: "Tell my uncle that from that day nothing binds us together, tell the imam I renounce his religion." Thus, amidst such controversies, it is Biram, the king's son who is chosen to deliver his sister. Biram recognizes the honor which is conferred upon him. He says to the king: "Father, thank you. I thank you for having chosen me to avenge Dior. I'll bring her back." Biram leaves with the imam's blessings and the assurance that he will return victorious.

In the isolated area near the coast where the princess is kept prisoner, the Ceddo's griot announces Biram's coming. The

Ceddo prepares his bow and Biram his rifle. In the course of the armed confrontation, Biram does not have the time to reload his rifle and is killed by the Ceddo's arrow. The princess, seated on a liana hammock, powerlessly witnesses this sequence of events. Biram is then brought back to the village where he is given a religious burial by the imam and his followers.

Saxewar is now chosen to rescue the princess. This time the Ceddo puts his hat on a stick which stands up from behind a dune. Lured by the Ceddo's ruse, Saxewar shoots at the hat. As Saxewar thinks that the Ceddo is dead, he tells the princess: "Dior, the scoundrel is dead." The princess, however, wants to acknowledge fully Saxewar's victory over her abductor. She tells him: "Before leaving, I want to walk over his dead body." As both Saxewar and the princess come near him, the Ceddo jumps out of his hiding place and blinds Saxewar by throwing sand into his eyes. Saxewar, taken by surprise, fires a shot in the air. The Ceddo takes advantage of Saxewar's bewilderment and kills him with an arrow. Saxewar is brought back to the village where the imam refuses to bury him since he formerly refused to comply with Muslim religious precepts.

In the meantime, in the village, the Ceddo continue to appeal to the king to restore their right to religious and social freedom. Although the king is converted to Islam, he begins to resent the imam's interference with his rule as well as his increasing insubordination. He tells him: "Imam, you are going beyond your duty. Your duty is to conduct prayer not to make decisions." Later the king observes: "I've noticed that you never say king," to which the imam replies: "Allah is the only king I know and I live for him," thus vehemently disassociating himself from the king he formerly flattered to gain his trust. The imam's growing ascendancy is equally stressed by Madior, who tells his uncle: "Uncle, your throne is rotten. You are a goat which has been devoured by a hyena."

Soon after these dissensions between the king and the imam, the former dies, allegedly from a snake bite. The converted councilmen are appalled by the king's death since after Biram has been killed by the Ceddo, no other direct male descendant of the king can be enthroned. One of them sadly states: "The Tioub dynasty is ended. No son. What will we do?" Another firmly replies: "A woman on the throne is out of question." As they want to safeguard their privileges, the councilmen decide to support the imam's designs to the throne. The Ceddo are now afraid of the imam's reprisal and the holy war he envisions to force his opponents into submission. Ostracized and oppressed, the Ceddo's bitterness is reflected through the words of one of them: "The king, the white man, the imam, the princess are all lice who live on us." Soon, fighting the Ceddo and killing the Catholic priest, the imam's followers carry out their "holy war" and force the Ceddo's surrender by means of spears, bullets, and fire. The imam's authority is readily recognized by courtiers such as Jaraaf, who vainly attempts to protect his privileges under the new head man by vouching: "Imam, may your rule endure. People, today is a blessed day. . . . " Now the imam sets the bases of his theocracy by forbidding fetishism and imposing the teachings of the Koran as moral codes and rules of conduct. The Ceddo's heads are shaved, their amulets and beads are taken away. Men, women, and children are massively converted to Islam and given new names. Through parallel action, the viewers witness the princess who goes to bathe in the sea waters near the place of seclusion. Here, Sembene lingers, with his camera, on the majesty of her quasi-naked body as she slowly goes back to her hammock under the Ceddo's watchful eyes. She suspects neither her father's death nor his burial, which is taking place in the village. At one point, the princess goes to get a gourd of fresh water, which she offers to the Ceddo. The Ceddo, sensitive to her attention, comes near her until he realizes that she is using such apparent concern in an attempt to get close to him and pull his knife from his belt. As the princess's design is thwarted, she goes back to the hammock, sizing up her guard with her usual inscrutable look.

A Ceddo and his family, who prefer exile to conversion and who have left the village, pass by the place where the princess is kept prisoner. He breaks to the princess the news of her father's death. He asks her to join them rather than face the imam's rule. The princess declines such an offer, saying: "My mother is alone in the village. The one who brought me here will take me back." Now, upon learning the king's death, the Ceddo removes the string which limited the princess's whereabouts. His abduction becomes senseless now that the king is no longer alive. Soon, two mounted men sent by the imam appear in the distance. During the confrontation between the Ceddo and the imam's converts, the princess has a dreamlike vision. She imagines herself welcoming the Ceddo as he victoriously enters the village. She kneels in front of him and offers him fresh water to drink. The princess's vision is in sharp contrast with reality, since this time the Ceddo is unable to win over the imam's soldiers and is killed. The princess is brought back to the village by the imam's disciples. As she enters the village, she walks slowly with a fearless determination in her look. She walks in the direction of the imam's throne as the Ceddo grab the guards' rifles and immobilize them by holding the rifles to their mouths, ready for the ultimate sacrifice of their life to protect the princess. A long shadow precedes the princess who gets hold of a gun, grasping it from a stunned guard. She now faces the imam whose dwarflike size contrasts with his ascendancy and her physical tallness. He quietly and credulously follows her gestures without moving or trying to escape. The princess cold-bloodedly pulls the trigger of her rifle and kills the imam after which she turns around to face her father's former subjects. She walks quietly among the villagers. The last picture of the film is a freeze frame closeup of her inscrutable face as she looks straightforwardly into the audience's eyes.

Commenting about the abrupt ending of his film, Sembene stresses:

> What is shown in *Ceddo* is the matriarchal era before the coming of Islam. . . . With the coming of Islam, and you will notice this in *Ceddo*, women were assigned inferior roles in society. . . . Only the princess, when she comes, is found on the side of the men. When the princess kills the imam, it has great symbolic significance for modern Senegal. This action is contrary to present ideas and the role that women now hold. And this is the only reason the film has been banned in Senegal.[8]

In *Emitai*, the African woman instigates the men's action. In *Ceddo*, she goes a step forward, holds a gun, pulls the trigger, and liberates the villagers from their oppressor. If one sees her isolated action as being motivated by individual reasons, the princess is not a part of a collective body as in *Emitai*, although she actualizes the Ceddo's inherent wish to terminate the imam's rule. Her status as a princess dissociates her from the women in *Emitai* who mainly come from the hard-working peasantry. Yet it is interesting to note that both the women of *Emitai* and Princess Dior resist foreign imperialism with equally silent strength and determination.

To some critics, who might believe that social change should emerge from the bottom of a society—the masses—Sembene provides the following explanation as to the choice of his heroine: "as far as the heroine being a princess is concerned, one can belong to a privileged class and still participate in movements for justice and tolerance. . . . It's not always true that workers and peasants in Africa are the ones who make history. On the other hand, history in Africa is all too often made by the middle class, with its privileges to protect, who turn out to be conservative."[9]

Princess Dior, whose name is reminiscent of the great historical Senegalese figure Lat-Dior, who resisted French colonialism, is a political symbol of bravery and courage. She makes up for the weakness of her father and the men he used to rule. Through Princess Dior, Sembene stresses the influential role of the *lingueres* (princesses) and other women in Senegal's history.

The princess's character is complex. She reflects the arrogance of her class and demonstrates, at first, a profound dislike for her captor. She feels humiliated by the order imposed on her by one of her father's throne slaves. Yet soon, his audacity, ruse, and intelligence win her admiration. Later, after her father's death, she is ready to join with him in common efforts to depose the imam. Both her feelings of independence and womanly love are expressed in the dream sequence in which she offers him some water. With deference, she indicates that the Ceddo is now worthy of her love beyond all class restrictions and traditional African customs according to which, at that time, no unions were permissible across class lines. Furthermore, a woman's suitor and future husband was selected by the woman's family. One recalls that the princess was promised by her father to Saxewar, who had already accepted the terms of the dowry. But her father's death leads to the imaginary selection of the man whose life she is ready to share. In such respect, the feelings and intentions of the princess towards the Ceddo are clearly expressed through her imaginary gesture of kneeling in front of him while offering some water to quench his thirst. In Africa, when a man returns from a long journey or a long day of work, his wife often brings him water and in so doing kneels in front of him. Here then, contrary to what a non-African viewer might perceive, the princess's dream indicates that she foresees sharing the Ceddo's life. It is to be emphasized that her attitude reflects caring and by no means submission.

When the princess is given the opportunity to flee, her family solidarity and her honor prevent her from doing so. She does not want to abandon her mother, who is still in the village, and she might already intend to avenge her father's death. It is important to point out here that it is her status as a woman which allows her to accomplish her design. Regarding her as a subservient and dependent figure within a Muslim community, neither the villagers nor the imam have the slightest suspicion of her murderous intentions. As the king's successor, according to Muslim laws she probably would have been killed as a rival to the imam's power, had she been a man. As a woman, she is able to secure her ends and kill the usurper of the father's throne. The final shot of the film, in which she slowly walks amidst the men of her village, Ceddo and Muslims alike, indicates that she has used but also gone beyond her woman's status to ensure the villagers' freedom from the imam's rule. In her role as a woman, she has also been spared the imam's teachings and thus does not hesitate to kill a spiritual leader by aiming at his genitals and symbolically mutilating his power, which he had usurped from her father. With the imam's rule overturned, it is suggested through the final freeze frame shot of *Ceddo* that the princess will gratefully acknowledge the Ceddo's help and change their status instead of re-establishing her father's rule. Here, Sembene leaves way to various interpretations as he does concerning the princess's true intentions in killing the imam. Did she kill the imam to avenge her father's death and put an end to the imam's spiritual and political rule? Did she kill the imam because she had fallen in love with the Ceddo slain by the imam's emissaries? As in several of Sembene's other films, *Ceddo* invites the viewers to reconstruct and define their own conclusion.

Although her final act may be seen as an isolated and individual one, she succeeds, whatever her motives are, in changing a political and religious order alien to a traditional African political and religious system. Her individual initiative has a collective range and far-reaching consequences. As she walks among the villagers, any pre-existing class differentiation is erased. She is now the agent of their common liberation. In *Ceddo*, Sembene advocates in an epic tone the rediscovery of African identity, immortalizing the remembrance of its inspirational past in a chronicle celebrating the prowess of heroes to whom he confers present-day significance and an allegorical morality.

NOTES

1. From a series of interviews with Ousmane Sembene, conducted by the author in Senegal in 1978.
2. Ousmane Sembene, *Synopsis of Ceddo* (Dakar: Films Domirev, 1978).
3. Ibid.
4. From a lecture delivered by Sembene at Howard University, Washington, D.C., 19 February 1978.
5. Guy Hennebelle, "Les Cinémas Africains en 1972," *L'Afrique Littéraire et Artistique*, n. 20 (1972), p. 206. Author's translation.
6. Sembene's lecture at Howard University, 1978.
7. Saxewar's coming on horseback stresses his high social status as well as his bravery. In pre-colonial sub-Saharan Africa, mostly the people belonging to the nobility and/or the warrior's class (who were fighting on horseback) were entitled to horses. Then, horses were rare and thus highly praised. Their usually short life in tropical African climates was due to the tsetse fly.
8. Ousmane Sembene, interviewed in *Seven Days*, 10 March 1978, p. 27.
9. Ibid.

10
CONCLUSION

In his films, Sembene systematically discards any escapist and "Tarzanistic" images of Africa. Instead, the Senegalese director addresses the multiple complexities of Africa's evolving societies. These include the vulnerability of average citizens coping with forces beyond their control, limited resources, new techniques of communication, and government bureaucracy. Sembene's films explore the difficulties common people face because of poverty and illiteracy, the condition of women and of the family, the question of freedom, authority, and the role of the community in individual's lives. The films also stress the misdeeds of colonialism and neo-colonialism and the cultural alienation that has ensued. They denounce the exploitation of people by some of the new Senegalese elite. Throughout his works, Sembene deals with the conflictive dichotomy between African traditions and new values inherited from the West. Generally, he illustrates a crisis situation that leads to a new awareness in both his protagonists and viewers. While doing so, the filmmaker does not limit his interest to the examination of acute contemporary problems but also uses Africa's past in order to shed light on its present. This is why a study of Sembene's films leads to a better understanding of African societies.

In presenting to his compatriots a large array of social issues according to his world view, Sembene uses a realistic approach to film. Since his plots are usually based on facts, he has a definite affinity for a clear film language that remains as close as possible to the reality of the stories he narrates. Sembene's apparent preference for realism, however, does not exclude symbolism, for it is as a griot that the filmmaker utilizes the film experience. Scrutinizing the past, evaluating the present, and suggesting the framework for a future Africa, Sembene pursues the didactic role of the griot as the bard, the historian, and the moralist of his society.

Sembene's motion pictures should not be studied in isolation from other world trends in film. However, specific standards, deriving from the context in which they were created, should be applied to his films. Sembene's works should be judged within the context of African aesthetics, for they derive from the African tradition of art as a functional medium. In Africa, art has always been functional and part of people's lives. So is Sembene's cinema.

This study of Sembene does not by any means imply that he is the only African filmmaker worthy of attention. He is, nevertheless, the one who has accomplished the most and has been the most influential participant in the definition of both African film aesthetics and ethics. He has successfully adapted film, a primarily Western medium, to the needs, pace, and rhythm of African culture. It is to be observed that he has done so without exhausting all the technical possibilities of film, for he has placed more interest in its storytelling capabilities.

Sembene is frequently called the father of African cinema. His works, talks, and writings have had a lasting impact on other African and Third World filmmakers. He has proven to them that meager financial and technical resources in a realm controlled by Western monopolies have not necessarily hampered creativity and that, on the contrary, a new film language could be created and appreciated worldwide.

Sembene's films are primarily intended for African audiences but they provide as well, for the world at large, significant examples of black Africa's young cinema. In less than two decades, with filmmakers like Sembene, such cinema has become the most recent expression of black African art.

APPENDIX 1
SEMBENE: A BIOGRAPHICAL SKETCH

1923   Born 1 January 1923 in Ziguinchor, Senegal. Of Lebou origin and Muslim extraction. His father was a fisherman. After his parents' divorce, Sembene spent early years divided between his father in Casamance and his uncles. Was greatly influenced by Abdou Rahmane Diop, his mother's oldest brother, a Marsassoum school teacher and the author of writings on Islam.

1935   Death of Abdou Rahmane Diop. Sembene went to Dakar where he began to prepare for an exam (*Certificat d'Etudes*) which he never took. A fist fight with his school principal caused the youth to drop out of school at fourteen.

1938   Developed an interest in masonry, which occupied his daylight hours, while evenings were spent at movies. Period marked by religious mysticism. Sembene devoutly pursued Muslim faith. First contacts with local union leaders. On weekends, Sembene enjoyed listening to griots who taught him about Africa's rich epic past and familiarized him with traditional storytelling techniques. Participation in the activities of an amateur theater troupe.

1942   Joined the French colonial troops. Fought in Africa and Europe as an artillery man.

1946   Demobilized in Dakar. Subsequent participation in the

	Dakar-Niger railroad workers' strike for better wages and improved working conditions (October 1947–March 1948).
1948	Started working as a longshoreman in Marseilles, where he took part in the political and cultural activities of African students. Joined workers' union (CGT). Took vehement stand against the French colonial presence in Indochina. Beginning of growing interest in black American and Caribbean writers like Richard Wright and Claude McKay. Desire to bring African literature to forefront.
1951–1954	Trips to Denmark. Time devoted to painting and poetry writing.
1956	Publication of first novel, *Le Docker Noir* (The Black Dockworker), reflecting Sembene's varied experiences as an African worker in France.
1957	Publication of novel, *O Pays Mon Beau Peuple* (O My Country, My Beautiful People), about the return of a Senegalese war veteran to his native village and his self-imposed mission of organizing the peasants and modernizing their farming techniques. Travelled to the U.S.S.R.
1958	Met W.E.B. Dubois at the First Congress of African and Asiatic Writers in Tashkent. Subsequent trips to China and North Vietnam.
1960	Publication of *Les Bouts de Bois de Dieu* (God's Bits of Wood), an outgrowth of Sembene's involvement in the Dakar-Niger strike, a novel which launched his literary career. Contacts with French writers such as Paul Eluard, Louis Aragon, Jean-Paul Sartre, and Simone de Beauvoir. Mingled with black writers like Aimé Césaire, Léon Damas, Camara Laye, Mongo Beti, Bernard Dadié, Ferdinand Oyono, and others.
1961	Returned to Africa. Realized the limited impact of African literature in Africa. Became convinced that a much greater access to African masses could be achieved through film. During a subsequent visit to Paris, Sembene met with film critics and filmmakers Georges Sadoul, Jean Rouch, and Louis Daquin. Upon Daquin's advice, Sembene sought financial aid from France, the U.S.S.R., Canada, the U.S., Poland, and Czechoslova-

	kia for training in filmmaking. Publication of a collection of short stories, *Voltaïque* (Tribal Scars).
1962	After a favorable reply from the U.S.S.R., Sembene spent a year studying at the Gorki Studio in Moscow, under the tutelage of cinematographers Donskoi and Guerassimov.
1963	Published *L'Harmattan*. This novel interweaves the lives and experiences of numerous characters in a fictitious country. Its setting is amidst a political upheaval which closely parallels De Gaulle's Referendum of 1958 in France. Made a short film, *L'Empire Sonhrai* (The Sonhrai Empire). Release of Sembene's first significant film, *Borom Sarret*.
1964	Publication of the short story, *Vehi-Ciosane*, and novel, *Le Mandat* (The Money Order). Release of film, *Niaye*.
1966	*Vehi-Ciosane* and *Le Mandat* are acclaimed as best works by an African writer at the First International Festival of Negro Arts in Dakar. Release of *La Noire De* (Black Girl), a film based on a story from *Voltaïque*.
1967	Served as one of the official judges at the Cannes Film Festival.
1968	Release of *Mandabi* (The Money Order).
1969	Made two films for two European television stations. Reactivated work in masonry to improve his home in Dakar at Yoff.
1970	Release of film, *Taw*.
1971	Release of film, *Emitai*.
1972	Was instrumental in the creation of *Kaddu* (The Voice), a Dakar newspaper in Wolof.
1973	Published novel, *Xala*.
1974	Marriage to Carrie Moore.
1975	Release of film, *Xala*.
1976	Release of *Ceddo*.
1981	Publication of a two-volume novel *Le Dernier de l'Empire* (The Last of the Empire), about a constitutional *coup d'état* organized by a fictitious Senegalese president.
1982	Final touches brought to a screenplay about Samori Touré.

APPENDIX 2
SEMBENE'S FILMS: CREDITS

L'EMPIRE SONHRAI 1963, in French

A documentary on the Sonhrai empire directed by Ousmane Sembene and produced by the Malian government. This film has never been commercially distributed.

BOROM SARRET 1963, in French

Director: Ousmane Sembene
Screenplay: Ousmane Sembene
Photography: Christian Lacoste
Assistant Director: Ibrahima Barro
Editing: André Gaudier
Production Companies: Les Actualités Françaises, Films Domirev
20 minutes; 35 mm; black and white.

Cast

The Cartman: Abdoulaye Ly
The Horse: Albouarah

Although this appendix focuses on credits, a film summary is provided here for films such as *L'Empire Sonhrai*, *Niaye*, and *Taw*, which are not included in the section of this book devoted to the interpretive study of Sembene's most significant films. *Borom Sarret*, *Black Girl*, *Mandabi*, *Taw*, *Emitai*, *Xala*, and *Ceddo* are distributed (in 16 mm) in the U.S. by New Yorker Films, 43 West 61st Street, New York, N. Y. 10023.

NIAYE 1964, in French

Director: Ousmane Sembene
Screenplay: Ousmane Sembene
Story based on *Véhi Ciosane*, a short story by Ousmane Sembene.
Photography: Georges Caristan
Assistant Director: Ibrahima Barro
Editing: André Gaudier
Production Companies: Les Films Domirev, Actualités Françaises
35 minutes; 35 mm; black and white.

Cast

The Griot: Sow
The Woman Griot: Astou N'Diaye
The Mother: Mame Dia
The Soldier: Modou Sene
The Village People: The people of the village of Keur Haly Sarrata

Film Summary

A thirteen-year-old girl is discovered to be pregnant. This revelation causes disruptions in her small Senegalese village. Her mother questions her but the young girl refuses to reveal who is responsible for her pregnancy. An alien field worker is believed to be the father of the expected child. Although he denies the accusation, he is banished from the village. Later, the village discovers that it is the girl's father who is the culprit. A tragic sequence of events ensues. The father is killed by his son, a former soldier in the French army, and the young girl's mother commits suicide. The young girl and her newborn child are subsequently rejected from their community, whose honor has been tarnished. The village is anxious to keep its dignity and the secret of these tragedies is not disclosed to the French administrator. This tragic story is related by the village griot.

BLACK GIRL (LA NOIRE DE . . .) 1966, in French

Director: Ousmane Sembene
Screenplay: Ousmane Sembene
Story from *Voltaïque*, a collection of short stories by Ousmane Sembene.

Photography: Christian Lacoste
Assistant Directors: Ibrahima Barro, Pathé Diop
Editing: André Gaudier
Production Companies: Les Actualités Françaises, Films Domirev
60 minutes; 35 mm; black and white.

Cast

Diouana: Thérèse M'Bissine Diop
The Young Man: Momar Nar Sene
Madame: Anne-Marie Jelinck
Master: Robert Fontaine
Boy with Mask: Ibrahima

MANDABI (THE MONEY ORDER) 1968, in Wolof

Director: Ousmane Sembene
Screenplay: Ousmane Sembene
Story from *The Money Order*, short story by Ousmane Sembene.
Photography: Paul Soulignac
Assistant Director: Ababacar Samb
Editing: Bérnard Lefèbre
Sound: Henri Moline
Production Companies: Comptoir Français du Film, Films Domirev
105 minutes; 35 mm; color.

Cast

Ibrahima Dieng: Makhourédia Gueye
First Wife: Younousse N'Diaye
Second Wife: Issa Niang
The Imam: Serigne Sow
The Shopkeeper: Moustapha Touré
The Postman: Medoune Faye
The Nephew: Moussa Diouf
Ibrahima Dieng's Sister: Thérèse Bass
The Water Seller: Christophe N'Doulabia

TAW 1970, in Wolof

Director: Ousmane Sembene
Screenplay: Ousmane Sembene

Photography: Georges Caristan
Assistant Director: Pap Sow
Editing: Mawa Gaye
Music: Diabaré Samb
Sound: El Hadji M'Bow
Production Manager: Paulin Soumanou Vieyra
Production Companies: Broadcasting Film Commission, National Council of the Church of Christ
24 minutes; 16 mm; color.

Cast

Amadou Dieng, Mamadou M'Bow, Fatim Diagne, Coumba Mané, Yoro Cissé, Mamadou Diagne, Christophe N'Doulabia.

Film Summary

Taw is twenty and is still living in his father's house where food is sometimes scarce. Although he has been to school, he is unable to find a job, a situation which his father wrongly attributes to laziness. One morning, after an argument with his father, he leaves home to meet a group of other unemployed young men. Together they go to see if they can possibly find jobs in the harbor. In order to gain access to the harbor, a guard must be paid. After getting the necessary funds from his girlfriend, Taw goes back to the harbor and learns that all the work has been assigned. Taw sadly wanders through the streets of Dakar pondering over the poor job market in Senegal, ten years after its independence. After his return home, his girlfriend comes and surprises him with the news that she has just been thrown out of her house by her father because of her pregnancy. The young man decides to leave his parents' home and start a life for himself and his family to be. After having formerly denied his responsibility in his girlfriend's pregnancy, he announces that he will marry her and enter the difficult world of adulthood.

EMITAI 1971, in Diola and French

Director: Ousmane Sembene
Screenplay: Ousmane Sembene
Photography: Georges Caristan
Assistant Director: Pap Sow
Editing: Gilbert Kikoine

Sound: El Hadj M'Bow
Production Manager: Paulin Soumanou Vieyra
Production Company: Films Domirev
95 minutes; 35 mm; color.

Cast

The Commandant: Robert Fontaine
The Lieutenant: Michel Renaudeau
The Colonel: Pierre Blanchard
The Sergeant: Andoujo Diahou
The Corporal: Fodé Cambay
The Villagers: Thérèse M'Bissine Diop, Ibou Camara, Ousmane Camara, Josephy Diatta, Dji Niassebanor, Sibesalang, Kalifa

XALA 1974, in French and Wolof

Director: Ousmane Sembene
Screenplay: Ousmane Sembene
Story based on *Xala*, a novel by Ousmane Sembene.
Photography: Georges Caristan
Editing: Florence Eymon
Sound: El Hadji M'Bow
Production Manager: Paulin Soumanou Vieyra
Production Companies: Société Nationale de Cinématographie, Films Domirev
116 minutes; 35 mm; color.

Cast

El Hadji Abdoukader Beye: Thierno Leye
First Wife: Seun Samb
Second Wife: Younousse Seye
Third Wife: Dieynaba Dieng
Rama, the Daughter: Miriam Niang
Gorgui, the Old Beggar: Douta Seck
Secretary: Fatim Diagne
The Client: Moustapha Touré
The Chauffeur: Ilimane Sagnan
The President: Makhourédia Gueye
The Minister: Abdoulaye Seck

The Deputy Minister: Doudou Gueye
The Banker: Farba Sarr

CEDDO 1976, in Wolof

Director: Ousmane Sembene
Screenplay: Ousmane Sembene
Photography: Georges Caristan
Editing: Florence Eymon
Music: Manu Dibango
Production Company: Films Domirev
120 minutes; 35 mm; color.

Cast

Princess Dior: Tabara N'Diaye
Madir Faim Fall: Moustapha Yade
The Kidnapper: Ismaila Diagne
The Imam: Goure
The King: Makhourédia Gueye
Jaraaf: Oumar Gueye
Prince Biram: Mamadou Diagne
Saxewar: Nar Modou Sene
Diogamay: Ousmane Camara
A Ceddo Renamed Ibrahima: Ousmane Sembene

APPENDIX 3
SEMBENE'S IMPACT ON FILMMAKING

FILM CRITICS

"If Ousmane must be thanked for what he creates, he must also understand that he is far from being alone: his action will be joined with that of all men burning for justice." Bass, "Je ne milite dans aucun parti, je milite à travers mon oeuvre, nous affirme Ousmane Sembene," *Dakar-Matin* (11–12 April 1966), p. 1. Author's translation.

". . . To put on the very weak film [*Black Girl*] of a young Senegalese director is a disastrous and paternalistic attitude; it can only bring harm to the young Senegalese who are starting to make films." Jacques Bontemps, "Semaine de la Critique à Cannes: La Noire de . . . de Ousmane Sembene," *Cahiers du Cinéma*, n. 179 (1966), p. 48. Author's translation.

"*Le Mandat (Mandabi)* . . . a plea for progress and development, should do well and establish its director as the staunchest representative of the young African cinema, if not that of the Third World." Bara Diouf, "*Le Mandat*, film d'Ousmane Sembene," *Dakar-Matin* (7 December 1968), p. 8. Author's translation.

"While the problems of 'Black Girl' remain uneven and unresolved, Mr. Sembene gives us a pointed and poignant view of the struggle for existence in Dakar's lower depths in the 19-minute 'Borom Sarret.' . . .

"The films, which are Mr. Sembene's first efforts and date back to 1966, are not landmarks of technique. But they put a sharp, bright focus on an emerging, once dark African area and on a forceful talent with fine potentials." A. H. Weiler, "Screen: 2 from Senegal," *New York Times* (13 January 1969), p. 31.

"Sembene's new film [*Emitai*] has been marred by censorship but what we can see of it is a masterpiece—a new style of film, unlike the "Musée de L'Homme" documentary quality that hinders *Mandabi* stylistically, and totally different from all western manners of story-telling on film. Few films cannot be related to other films in their story or in their style; Sembene's *Emitai* can be related to Sophocle's *Antigone* in its story, but not to any film in its style. . . . " Lyle Pearson, "Four Years of African Film," *Film Quarterly* (Spring 1973), p. 46.

"Ousmane Sembene's *Emitai* demands patience and a little tolerance. Its lack of form and polish are only too apparent. But its political passion in portraying the exploitation of the Senegal people by the French in the Second World War cannot be dismissed and certainly not patronized." Margaret Hinxman, "So Many Children . . . " *Sunday Telegraph* (1 July 1973), p. 18.

"Unfortunately the surface flummery of much of Sembene's comedy—the goggling buffoonishness of the hero, the domestic tiffs that continually turn into a neighborhood shouting match—is over-indulged, and for all the professed seriousness of the director's satire, *The Money Order* is too heavily padded with weary folk comedy. . . . " Richard Combs, "Jodorowsky's Carnival of Cruelty," *The Times* (26 October 1973), p. 15.

"The Sembene movies released in this country have been all relentlessly depressing, but they flowed rhythmically and naturally from their director's own distinctly black sensibility. In the somber *Borom Sarret*, in the distressingly cerebral *Mandabi* and in the masterpiece of suicidal despair, *Black Girl*, Sembene creates characters victimized not only by white hypocrisies and injustices but by black ones as well." Donald Bogle, *Toms, Coons, Mulattoes, Mammies and Bucks* (New York: Viking Press, 1973), p. 243.

"Ousmane Sembene is Africa's major film talent. . . . Sembene's work (*Mandabi*) marks the emergence of a truly indigenous African cinema." Amos Vogel, *Film as a Subversive Art* (New York: Random House, 1974), p. 168.

"Nothing succeeds in his film world . . . heroes start off beaten, setbacks reside in them from the very beginning and their defeat comes ineluctably as the final stage of a fall into hopelessness. . . . " Le Cyclope, "*Xala*, Rut Barre d'Ousmane Sembene," *Le Soleil* (27 February 1975), p. 11. Author's translation.

"*Xala* is the work of one of the most remarkable artists in the world, the Senegalese novelist-filmmaker Ousmane Sembene." Jack Kroll, "The World on Film," *Newsweek* (13 October 1975), p. 103.

"*Xala* makes history, as the first black African feature film to be shown commercially in Britain. . . . Some aspects of the narrative belong to a story-telling tradition strange to the West. The humiliation of the end is horrid and bizarre; the introduction of allegory, and of El Hadji's nemesis in the person of a beggar who out of the blue reveals that years before he has been ruined by the business man's villainy, seems arbitrary to a Western viewer; but the character, the comedy, the satire at the expense of a corrupt and pretentious bourgeoisie is instantly and wickedly effective." David Robinson, "The Nasty Spell of Success," *The Times* (5 November 1976), p. 9.

"It must be admitted that, until this point, the value of Sembene Ousmane's films lay more in their themes, their documentary approach, their humor, their lucidity, and also their political courage than in film language. Thus, *Ceddo* marks a true turning point and a notable transformation in the filmmaker's career. Sembene Ousmane had been making "Western" films about his country. With *Ceddo*, he establishes deep roots in this country, its history and its culture." Barthélemy Amengual, "Ceddo, de Sembene Ousmane," *Positif*, n. 195–196 (1977), p. 83. Author's translation.

" . . . The Third World Euripides, Ousmane Sembene, analyzes in *Ceddo* the historical dynamics that led to the modern state of Senegal. Sembene's forte is the dramatic pageant, which seems almost primitive until you realize how evenly protagonists and antagonists are aligned and how wise his perceptions are about his country's social matrix." Tom Allen, "Pleasure over Pain: The Good, Better and Best," *Village Voice* (1 January 1979), p. 39.

"Ousmane Sembene possesses the vision of a committed cineaste of social change. All his films, self-critical ones, offer constructs to interpret the cultural jumble that covers Africa. In the Sembenian universe, film depicts not simply individuals bereft of context, caught between the traditional and the modern or the foreign and domestic, but shows the collision of two mutually exclusive symbol-systems, which serve their own set of icons and are equally arbitrary and mutually worthless to the other." Teshome Gabriel, "Xala: A Cinema of Wax and Gold," *Jump Cut*, n. 27 (1982), p. 31.

"Sembene Ousmane, one of the doyens of sub-Saharan African cinema . . . Senegal's leading filmmaker and one of the brightest talents in the continent's struggling film industry." Howard Schissel, "Sembene Ousmane: Film-Maker," *West Africa* (18 July 1983), p. 1665.

FILMMAKERS

"It is after seeing *Borom Sarret* by Ousmane Sembene that I decided to become a filmmaker." Cheikh Ngaido Bah, interviewed by the author, Senegal, 1978.

"Sembene and I do not always agree but I have a lot of admiration for him. He believes in what he does. . . . He has had an impact on the style and themes of African cinema . . . he has already influenced a few Senegalese filmmakers. He was the first one to make a film in Wolof and since then many filmmakers have followed in his footsteps." Yves Diagne, interviewed by the author, Senegal, 1978.

"Sembene is a significant filmmaker but I have the feeling that his films (except for *Emitai* and *Ceddo*) repeat what he did in *Mandabi* or *Black Girl*. They show similar problems, there is no evolution in his ideas. His technical approach remains the same. He does not use new available film techniques." Niagane, interviewed by the author, Senegal, 1978.

"A critical view of contemporary African societies and the conflicts between tradition and modernity are found in all African films. What characterizes Sembene is his search for thematic diversity. Each of his films rests on one aspect of Senegalese life." Paulin Soumanou Vieyra, interviewed by the author, Senegal, 1978.

"As far as we are concerned, Sembene is a monument. . . . He has entered our history. . . . It is mainly his combativity which has had an impact on me. He is a man of iron strength and Africa needs men like him." Souleymane Cissé, African Film and Filmmakers Lecture Series, Howard University, Washington, D.C., 16 September 1983.

"We all admire his willpower. Yet, in terms of film language, I do not feel I have been influenced by Sembene." Nkieri Ngunia-Wawa, African Film and Filmmakers Lecture Series, Howard University, 16 September 1983.

Ousmane Sembene is not representative of African cinema because African cinema is much broader than Ousmane Sembene. Med Hondo or Haile Gerima, for example, have approaches to film which are different from Sembene's. But, by his position in time and history, he is one of the earlier filmmakers engaging in the expression of African reality through the medium of film. Sembene is also the African filmmaker who is the most popularized by way of having received more exposure and so that his name is synonymous with African cinema in that context. . . . I would be influenced by Sembene in the sense that he sensitizes me to certain social issues. . . . *Xala* . . . allowed me to look at certain phenomena pertaining to colonialism, neo-colonialism, and other post-colonial activities. . . . " Abiyi Ford, interviewed by the author, Washington, D.C., 7 November 1983.

"I think that Sembene . . . is a forerunner because of the kinds of choices he has made. He is the kind of person who has tried to communicate through his culture. . . . He says to us 'be yourself and be proud of your cultures.' He has given me courage, confidence, and encouragement. I think that he has had an impact on me and on a lot of African filmmakers although they may, egotistically, not admit it." Haile Gerima, interviewed by the author, Washington, D.C., 13 November 1983.

BIBLIOGRAPHY

Agel, Henri. *Métaphysique du Cinéma*. Paris: Payot, 1976.
Allen, Tom. "Pleasure over Pain: The Good, Better and Best." *Village Voice*, 1 January 1979, p. 39.
Amengual, Barthélemy. "Ceddo, de Sembene Ousmane." *Positif*, n. 195–196, 1977, p. 83.
Arnheim, Rudolf. *Film as Art*. Berkeley and Los Angeles: University of California Press, 1957.
Asheim, Lester. "From Book to Film." *The Quarterly of Film, Radio and Television*, vol. 6, n. 3, 1952, p. 264.
Aumont, Jacques, and Sylvie Pierre. "Huit Fois Deux." *Cahiers du Cinéma*, n. 206, 1968, pp. 30–32.
Balandier, Georges, and Jacques Maquet. *Dictionary of Black African Civilization*. New York: Léon Amiel, 1974.
Banham, Martin, with Clive Wake. *African Theater Today*. London: Pitman Publishing, 1976.
Bass. "Je ne milite dans aucun parti, je milite à travers mon oeuvre, nous affirme Ousmane Sembene." *Dakar-Matin*, 11–12 April 1966, p. 1.
Blair, Dorothy S., translator. *Birago Diop's Tales of Amadou Koumba*. London: Oxford University Press, 1966.
Boggs, Joseph M. *The Art of Watching Films*. Menlo Park, Calif.: Benjamin/Cummings Publishing Co., 1978.
Bogle, Donald. *Toms, Coons, Mulattoes, Mammies and Bucks*. New York: Viking Press, 1973.

Bontemps, Jacques. "Semaine de la Critique à Cannes: La Noire de . . . de Ousmane Sembene." *Cahiers du Cinéma*, n. 179 (1966), p. 48.

Capdenac, Michel. "Le Mandat, film sénégalais de Sembene Ousmane." *Les Lettres Françaises*, n. 1259, 1968, p. 22.

Cham, Mbye B. "Oral Narrative Patterns in the Work of Ousmane Sembene." Unpublished paper, 1982, pp. 1–27.

Combs, Richard. "Jodorowsky's Carnival of Cruelty." *The Times* 26 October 1973, p. 15.

Cripps, Thomas. *Black Film as Genre*. Bloomington: Indiana University Press, 1979.

Crowley, Daniel J., editor. *African Folklore in the New World*. Austin: University of Texas Press, 1977.

Cyclope, Le. "*Xala*, Rut Barre d'Ousmane Sembene." *Le Soleil*, 27 February 1975, p. 11.

Delmas, Jean and Ginette. "Ousmane Sembene: Un Film est un Débat." *Jeune Cinéma*, n. 99, December 1976–January 1977, pp. 13–17.

Diack, Moktar. "Emitai or Africa Arisen." *Young Cinema and Theatre*, n. 4, 1972, pp. 27–29.

Diouf, Bara. "Le Mandat, film d'Ousmane Sembene." *Dakar-Matin*, 7 December 1968, p. 8.

Fanon, Frantz. *The Wretched of the Earth*. New York: Grove Press, 1979.

Flatley, Guy. "Senegal Is Senegal, Not Harlem." *New York Times*, 2 November 1969, p. D17.

Gabriel, Teshome. "Xala: A Cinema of Wax and Gold." *Jump Cut*, n. 27, 1982, pp. 31–33.

Ghali, Noureddine. "Ousmane Sembene." *Cinéma 76*, n. 208, 1976, pp. 83–95.

Haffner, Pierre. *Essai sur les Fondements du Cinéma Africain*. Abidjan-Dakar: Les Nouvelles Editions Africaines, 1978.

Hennebelle, Guy. "Socially Committed or Exotic Films from French-Speaking Africa." *Young Cinema and Theatre*, n. 3, 1970, pp. 24–33.

———. "Les Cinémas Africains en 1972." *L'Afrique Littéraire et Artistique*, n. 20, 1972, pp. 1–371.

Hennebelle, Guy, and Catherine Ruelle. "Cinéastes d'Afrique Noire." *L'Afrique Littéraire et Artistique*, n. 49, 1978, pp. 1–192.

Hinxman, Margaret. "So Many Children. . . . " *Sunday Telegraph*, 1 July 1973, p. 18.

Hutchinson, Joyce A., editor. *Birago Diop—Contes Choisis*. Cambridge: Cambridge University Press, 1967.

Kroll, Jack. "The World on Film." *Newsweek*, 13 October 1975, pp. 103–4.
Leab, Daniel J. *From Sambo to Superspade*. Boston: Houghton Mifflin Co., 1976.
Lebel, Jean Patrick. *Cinéma et Idéologie*. Paris: Editions Sociales, 1971.
Marcorelles, Louis. "Ousmane Sembene, Romancier, Cinéaste, Poète." *Les Lettres Françaises*, n. 1177, 12 April 1967, p. 24.
Masson, Alain. "Mascarade à Dakar." *Positif*, n. 182, 1976, pp. 54–56.
N'Diaye, Alphonse Raphaël. "Les Traditions Orales et la Quête de l'Identité Culturelle." *Présence Africaine*, n. 114, 1980, pp. 3–17.
N'Doye, Aicha, and Sarah Kala, contributors. *La Civilisation de la Femme dans la Tradition Africaine*. Paris: Présence Africaine, 1975.
Pearson, Lyle. "Four Years of African Film." *Film Quarterly*, Spring 1973, pp. 42–47.
Pfaff, Françoise. "Toward a New Era in Cinema." *New Directions*, vol. 4, n. 3, 1977, pp. 28–30.
———. "Notes on Cinema." *New Directions*, vol. 6, n. 1, 1979, pp. 26–29.
———. "Ousmane Sembene: His Films, His Art." *Black Art*, vol. 3, n. 3, 1979, pp. 29–36.
———. "Entretien avec Ousmane Sembene: A Propos de Ceddo." *Positif*, n. 235, 1980, pp. 54–57.
———. "Myths, Traditions and Colonialism in Ousmane Sembene's Emitai." *CLA Journal*, vol. 24, n. 3, March 1981, pp. 336–46.
———. "Three Faces of Africa: Women in Xala." *Jump Cut*, n. 27, 1982, pp. 27–31.
Pommier, Pierre. *Cinéma et Développement en Afrique Noire Francophone*. Paris: Pédone, 1974.
Robinson, David. "The Nasty Spell of Success." *The Times*, 5 November 1976, p. 9.
Rouch, Jean. "L'Afrique entre en Scène." *Le Courrier de l'Unesco*, n. 3, 1962, pp. 10–15.
Sartre, Jean-Paul. *Black Orpheus*. Paris: Présence Africaine, 1976.
Schissel, Howard. "Sembene Ousmane: Film-Maker." *West Africa*, 18 July 1983, pp. 1665–66.
Sèche, Alphonse. *Les Noirs*. Paris: Payot, 1919.
Sembene, Ousmane. *L'Harmattan*. Paris: Présence Africaine, 1963.
———. *Tribal Scars*. London: Heinemann, 1974.
———. "Filmmakers and African Culture." *Africa*, n. 71, 1977, p. 80.
———. "Seven Days Interview: Sembene." *Seven Days*, 10 March 1978, pp. 26–27.

―――. *Synopsis of Ceddo*. Dakar: Films Domirev, 1978.
―――. "Entretien avec Sembene Ousmane." *Les 2 Ecrans*, n. 12, 1979, pp. 19–21.
Tarratt, Margaret. "The Money Order." *Films and Filming*, vol. 20, n. 4, 1974, pp. 45–48.
Thomas, Louis Vincent. *Les Diolas*. Dakar: IFAN, 1959.
Traoré, Bakary. *The Black African Theater and Its Social Functions*. Ibadan, Nigeria: Ibadan University Press, 1972.
Vaughan, J. Koyinde. "Africa South of the Sahara and the Cinema." *Présence Africaine*, n. 14–15, 1957, pp. 210–21.
Vieyra, Paulin Soumanou. "Le Deuxième Festival Cinématographique de Tachkent." *Présence Africaine*, n. 83, 1972, pp. 86–91.
―――. *Sembène Ousmane Cinéaste*. Paris: Présence Africaine, 1972.
Vogel, Amos. *Film as a Subversive Art*. New York: Random House, 1974.
Weaver, Harold. "Interview with Ousmane Sembene." *Issue*, vol. 2, n. 4, 1972, pp. 58–64.
Weiler, A. H. "Screen: 2 from Senegal." *New York Times* 13 January 1969, p. 31.
Yondo, Elolongué Epanya. *La Place de la Littérature Orale en Afrique*. Paris: La Pensée Universelle, 1976.

INDEX

Abdessalam, Shadi, 70
Abikanlou, Pascal, 12, 14
Abusuan, 13
Adja Tio, 14
African art, 122, 180
Africa Texas Style, 7
Afrique 50, 6
Afrique en Piste, L', 12
Afrique-sur-Seine, 10
Afro-American Films (AFRAM), 21
Allégret, Marc, 6
Allassane, Mustapha, 12, 14, 16, 18, 31
Amanié, 16
Ame Perdue, 17
Ampaw, James King, 26
Animism, 57, 170
Ansah, Kwah, 26
Art, African, 122, 180
Au Pays des Pygmées, 6
Aventure en France, 17
Aw, Tidiane, 16
Ayouma, 16

Baara, 17, 25
Bah, Cheikh Ngaido, 15
Baks, 15
Ballets de la Forêt Sacrée, Les, 13
Balogun, Ola, 26
Bambara, 25
Barry, Sekoumar, 12
Bassori, Timité, 12
Bathily, Moussa, 12, 25
Benin, 12, 17, 23
Beye, Ben Diogaye, 13, 15, 17
Bicots Nègres Vos Voisins, Les, 18
Bicycle Thief, 49
Black Girl, 113–25; actors in, 53, 55–56; budget, 76, 77; film technique, 49, 52; irony in, 71, 72, 74; and lyricism, 69; Sembene in, 56; soundtrack, 62, 66, 68; symbolism in, 58
Borom Sarret, 99–111; budget, 76–77; characters, 34–35; as comedy, 74; film technique in, 49, 50–51; and French sponsors, 114–15; griot in, 32; and

Borom Sarret (continued)
  lyricism, 69; plot, 15, 37; soundtrack, 62–63, 64, 67; symbolism in, 52
Brosse, La, 15
Burroughs, Edgar Rice, 4

Cabascabo, 18, 25
Cabral, Amilcar, 54, 60, 159, 160
Camara, Amadou S., 17
Cameroon, 13, 15, 16, 17
Caristan, Georges, 77, 78
Ceddo, 165–77; budget, 20, 76; censorship in, 24; characters in, 38, 53, 55, 56; film technique, 48, 50–51, 52; griot in, 32, 33; and history, 12, 43, 46, 70–71; soundtrack, 62, 66–67, 68; symbolism in, 57, 70; themes of, 35, 37, 75; translations of, 25, 73; violence in, 69
Centre Inter Africain de Production de Films (CIPROFILMS), 23
Certificat, Le, 16
Chapeau, Le, 16
Cinq Jours d'une Vie, 15
Cissé, Souleymane, 15, 16, 17, 19, 20, 25
Clark, J. P., 10
Colonial Film Unit, 6
Compagnie Africaine Cinématographique Industrielle (COMACICO), 21, 22, 23
Concerto pour un Exil, 17
Congo, 11
Consortium Inter Africain de Distribution Cinématographique (CIDC), 23
Contras City, 17
Coulibaly, Diambéré Sega, 15
Cri du Muezzin, Le, 15
Croisière Noire, La, 5

Daybreak at Udi, 6
Deela, 12
De Gaulle, Charles, 74, 145
Delou Thyossane, 12
Den Muso, 16, 25
Destin, Le, 15
Diagne, Yves, 12
Diankha-Bi, 16
Diègue-Bi, 16, 22
Dikongue-Pipa, Jean Pierre, 13, 15
Diola, 25, 57, 120, 141, 142–43, 145–47
Djelli, 14
Dong, Pierre Marie, 16
Donskoi, Mark, 79
Doomi Ngatch, 14
Duparc, Henri, 13, 17, 25

Eisenstein, Sergei M., 60
Emitai, 141–47; characters in, 38, 53, 54–55, 73–74; directing of, 77; film technique in, 21, 48, 50–51, 52, 71; and history, 33, 43, 45, 168; plot, 12, 170, 174–75; soundtrack, 62, 64, 65, 67, 68, 70; symbolism in, 34, 35, 57–58, 60, 69; translation, 25
Empire Songhrai, L', 12
End of St. Petersburg, The, 49
En Résidence Surveillée, 17
Et la Neige n'était plus, 18
Etoile Noire, L', 16
Et Vint la Liberté, 12

Fadika, Kramo Lancine, 14
Fadjal, 14
Faye, Abdou Fary, 13
Faye, Safi, 14, 15, 17, 18, 25
Films, African: African art in, 12–13; alienation in, 10, 17, 18; animism in, 14, 35, 43; areas of, 9–10, 26; arranged marriages

in, 13; audiences, 21, 23, 180; beginnings, 10–11; bourgeoisie in, 16, 18; colonialism and, 10, 11, 18; and corruption, 13, 16, 17; didactic function of, 11; emigration in, 18; foreign monopolies and, 21, 22, 180; funding of, 20; and griots, 29; history in, 12; illegitimate children in, 13; illiteracy and, 11, 16; infrastructure and equipment of, 19, 21; Islam in, 14; juvenile delinquency in, 15, 18; and languages, 25; major themes, 9–19; migrant workers in, 18; nepotism in, 16; oral tradition, 31, 33, 39; political upheaval in, 17; polygamy in, 13; poverty in, 18; problems of, 19–25; prostitution in, 15; purpose, 11; religions in, 12; rural life in, 14, 15, 16, 18, 53; sports in, 12; style, 11; theft in, 15; traditions in, 12, 13; traditions vs. modernity in, 13, 14, 17, 18, 56; unemployment in, 15; urban life in, 15; women in, 16, 18, 68. *See also* Films, Sembene's

Films, Sembene's: actors, 38, 52–57; aesthetics, 80, 114, 180; and African art, 122; alienation in, 58, 99, 104, 106–8, 109, 113, 114, 116, 117–18, 121, 124, 130, 131, 132, 137–38, 145; amulets in, 59; animism in, 57, 101, 135, 142, 143, 147, 156; audiences, 177, 180; beggars in, 46, 55, 58, 60, 71, 103, 104, 110, 135, 150, 153, 160–62; bourgeoisie in, 47, 58, 59–60, 75, 104, 105, 134, 137, 139, 149, 150, 155, 156, 162, 179; bureaucracy in, 48, 127, 130, 133–35, 137, 139–40, 179; cars in, 59, 72, 154, 156; caste system in, 168; Catholicism in, 24, 59, 67, 166, 169, 173; censorship and, 24, 46, 75; children in, 52, 56, 72, 107, 121–22, 123, 124, 131–32, 133, 141, 151, 154; Christianity in, 165, 166, 168; civil servants in, 72; class consciousness in, 106, 175; clothing in, 60–61, 101, 105, 116, 120–21, 131, 134, 135, 138, 152, 154, 159, 170; and collective awareness, 124, 137, 145, 178, 179; colonialism in, 54, 55, 60, 114, 119, 123, 124, 133–34, 137, 141–44, 147, 159, 168, 179; as comedy and satire, 47, 59, 71–76, 150; corruption in, 17, 72, 75, 110, 134, 135–39, 150, 179; didactic elements, 180; education in, 109, 110, 154; emigration in, 125, 129; foreign legion in, 45; France in, 113, 116–17, 118–19, 120, 125, 131, 142, 144, 146, 157; French in, 64, 119, 130, 149, 154; funding of, 20, 47, 76; griots in, 62, 104, 106, 110, 180; heroes in, 125; history in, 46, 76, 142, 144, 165–67, 168, 169, 175, 179, 180; illiteracy in, 16, 35, 118, 129, 133, 179; incest in, 43; Islam in, 24, 55, 59, 61, 75, 100–01, 104, 105, 107, 108, 130, 131, 135–36, 149, 151, 156, 159, 162, 165–77; languages of 43–82, 99, 114, 156; lyricism and epic in, 69–71; male impotence in, 43, 71, 146, 152, 153, 159, 161; masks in, 58, 61, 70, 121–22, 123, 124–25, 165; money in, 101,

Films, Sembene's: (*continued*) 105, 107, 108, 118, 127, 129, 130, 131–38, 153; nature in, 69; neo-colonialism in, 55, 125, 158, 159, 179; nepotism in, 134, 140; oral tradition in, 62; Panafricanism in, 159; politicians in, 117; polygamy in, 130, 149, 151–54, 156–57, 158, 162; prostitution in, 108, 110; racism in, 118; realism in, 43–48, 166, 180; religion in, 50, 52, 59, 61, 110, 122, 124, 142, 143, 149; rituals, 122, 162; rural life in, 144, 145–46, 170; satire, 60, 67, 140; Senegalese audiences and, 47, 128; sex in, 118–19, 150, 152, 161; slavery in, 67, 117, 166, 168–70; social action in, 50, 137, 140, 147, 160, 175, 177; social awareness in, 139; social classes in, 118, 119, 129; soldiers and veterans in, 60, 64, 67, 74, 104, 105, 109, 116, 142, 143, 144, 147, 174; soundtrack in, 61–68, 99, 123; space and time in, 48–52; suicide in, 43, 113, 115, 119, 121, 122, 124, 125; symbolism, 57–61, 68, 72, 79, 107, 110, 116, 117, 119, 120, 122, 123, 124, 125, 129, 138, 150, 154, 155, 159, 160, 162, 176, 177, 180; theatrical elements in, 37, 38, 46, 70, 71, 128, 167; theft in, 110, 128, 136, 160; traditions in, 103, 107, 108, 116–17, 138, 142, 143, 146, 152, 156, 171, 174; traditions vs modernity, 36, 37, 99, 104, 107, 108–9, 124, 127, 131, 134, 138, 179; unemployment in, 102; urban life in, 15, 17, 48, 49, 99–111, 127–40, 156; violence in, 24, 69; women in, 16, 45, 61, 64, 72, 101, 102, 103, 107, 108, 110, 113–25, 130, 131, 133, 135, 141, 142, 145–46, 150, 151–59, 160–62, 170, 173–76, 179

Finyé, 17, 24

Fontaine, Robert, 53

400 Blows, The, 52

French, 20, 25, 99, 114. *See also* Films, Sembene's, French in

French Ministry of Cooperation, 20

F.V.V.A. (Femme, Voiture, Villa, Argent), 16

Gabon, 12, 13, 16, 17

Ganda, Oumarou, 13, 14, 18

Ganvié, Mon Village, 14

Garga M'Bossé, 15

Gentlemen de Cocody, Le, 7

Gerima, Haile, 9, 32

Gety Tey, 15

Ghana, 10, 26

Godard, Jean-Luc, 79

Grandes Chasses Africaines, Les, 6

Grand Magal à Touba, 12

Griots: in *Ceddo,* 170–71; definition, 29–30; Sembene as, 32–33, 34, 40, 180; as storytellers, 32–33, 38–39

Guinea, 12, 17, 20

Haggard, Sir Henry Rider, 4

Halilu, Alhaji Adamu, 26

Hatari, 7

Hausa, 25

Herbe Sauvage, L', 13

Hitchcock, Alfred, 57

Homme d'Ailleurs, L', 18

Homme du Niger, L', 4

Hondo, Med, 18, 20

Ilombe, 12
Ivory Coast, 12, 13, 15, 16, 17, 18, 23

Journée de Djibril N'Diaye, Paysan Sénégalais, La, 14

Kaba, Alkaly, 14
Kaddu Beykat, 14
Kamba, Sebastien, 12
Kamwa, Daniel, 13, 16
King Solomon's Mines, 4
Kodou, 13
Kola Djim, Mamadou, 14
Kossoko, Yaya, 16
Koula, Jean Louis, 14
Kouyaté, Djibril, 14

Lacoste, Christian, 77
Lambaaye, 16, 24
Lat-Dior, 175
Lewis, Etherelda, 4
London's Crown Film Unit, 6–7
Lumumba, Patrice, 60, 116
Luttes Casamançaises, 13

Maiga, Djinga-Reye, 16
Maldoror, Sarah, 6, 18
Mali, 12, 13, 14, 15, 16, 17, 23
Malle, Louis, 79
Mambety, Djibril Diop, 17
Mandabi, 127–40; and African people, 16, 142; characters in, 34, 35, 53, 55; as comedy, 71–72, 75; film technique, 37, 48–49, 50–51, 52, 79; griot in, 33; production of, 22, 77; Sembene in, 56; symbolism in, 59–60, 61, 75; and symbolism, 59–60, 61, 75; and tone, 38
Manga, Thomas Makoulet, 18
Marker, Chris, 6
Mauritania, 15, 18

M'Bala, Gnoan, 16
M'Baye, Ousmane William, 14
Meideros, Richard de, 17
Mensah, Charles, 12
Military Drill of the Kikuyu Tribes and Other Native Ceremonies, The, 5
Mr. Moses, 7
Mogambo, 4
Moi, ta Mère, 18
Mokouri, Urbain Dia, 17
Mon Stage en France, 18
Mory, Philippe, 17
Motion Picture Export Association of America (MPEAA), 21
Mouna ou le Rêve d'un Artiste, 17
Mummy, The, 70
Muna Moto, 13
Myths, 31, 142, 143, 146

Nagana, 4
Nationalité: Immigré, 18
Nation est Née, Une, 11
Ndiaye, Samba Felix, 15
N'Gassa, Jean Paul, 17
Ngugi, James, 10
Niaye, 32, 33, 48, 62, 67, 69, 71, 113
Niger, 12, 13, 14, 15, 16, 18
Nigeria, 10, 26, 43
Njangaan, 14
Notre Fille, 16
Nous Sommes Tous Coupables, 13
Nouveau Venu, Le, 17

O'Bali, 13
Office Béninois du Cinéma (OBECI), 23
Office Cinématographique du Mali (OCINAM), 23
Olusola, Segun, 26

Organisation Commune Africaine et Mauricienne (OCAM), 23
Owoo, Kwate Nee, 26

Passante, La, 17
Paysans Noirs, 4
Pétain, Philippe, 74, 89, 144
Pousse-Pousse, 13
Princes Noirs de St Germain des Prés, Les, 17
Prix de la Liberté, Le, 15
Pudovkin, Vsevlod I., 49, 60

Rançon d'une Alliance, La, 12
Réou Takh, 24
Resnais, Alain, 6
Retour de l'Aventurier, Le, 18
Retour de Tiéman, Le, 15
Réussite de Meithèbre, La, 16
Rewo Dande Mayo, 15
Roots of Heaven, 4–5
Rouch, Jean, 6, 8

Safari, 4
Safrana ou le Droit à la Parole, 18
Saitane, 14
Salute to the Queen, 6
Sam, Aryetey, 26
Samb, Ababacar, 13, 18, 20, 77
Samba Talli, 15
Sambizanga, 18
Samori, 60, 77, 159, 160
Sanders of the River, 4
Sang des Parias, Le, 14
Sarakholé, 25
Selbé, 15
Sembene, Ousmane: on acting, 53; as actor, 56–57; on amulets, 57; on *Ceddo,* 166, 174; censorship and, 24–25, 174; on comedy, 74; concern for Africa, 3, 8, 16–17, 43, 141, 160, 165, 175; as director and filmmaker, 15, 78, 79; education of, 19–20; filming problems, 20, 21, 76; film language of, 43–82; films' budgets, 76, 77; as griot, 29–42, 75, 79–80; on griot's role, 29, 40, 104; on history, 165, 167–69, 175; on *Mandabi,* 127–28; on music, 63–64, 65, 66; philosophy of, 36–37; on polygamy, 130; as rejecting traditional heroes, 125; on the relevance of film, 11, 39; statements about, 33, 72, 78, 128, 137, 139; on women, 160, 174; work resources and methods, 53–55, 76–78; use of clothing, 61; on *Xala,* 153, 158
Senegal, 10, 11, 12, 13, 14, 15, 16, 17, 18, 23, 24, 45, 46, 47, 48, 49, 59, 70, 76
Serigne Assane, 16
Senghor, Blaise, 12
Serer, 68, 165
Sey Seyeti, 13
Simb ou les Jeux du Faux Lion, 13
Sindiély, 13
Sita Bella, Thérèse, 13
Snows of Kilimanjaro, The, 4
Société d'Exploitation Cinématographique Africaine (SECMA), 21, 22
Société d'Importation de Distribution et d'Exploitation Cinématographique (SIDEC), 23
Société Ivoirienne du Cinéma (SIC), 23
Société Nationale du Cinéma (SNC), 23
Société Nationale du Cinéma Voltaïque (SONAVOCI), 23

Sokhona, Sidney, 18
Soleil O, 17
Sonhrai, 26
Sous le Signe du Vodoun, 12
South Africa, 10
Sow, Thierno, 14
Soyinka, Wole, 10
Statues Meurent Aussi, Les, 6
Storytelling, African, 29–40
Storytelling, Western, 32
Sur la Dune de la Solitude, 12
Sutherland, Efua, 10

Tam-Tam à Paris, 13
Tams Tams se sont Tus, Les, 17
Tarzan, 3, 4, 179
Tarzan and the Jungle Boy, 7
Taw, 25, 36, 52, 61, 77
Theodore Roosevelt's Journey to Africa, 5
Thiam, Momar, 13, 15, 31
Tirailleurs, 144, 146
Tiyabu Biru, 12, 25
Touki Bouki, 17
Toula ou le Génie des Eaux, 14
Trader Horn (1930), 4
Trader Horn (1973), 7
Tradition, oral, 30, 31, 32, 34, 39, 167
Traoré, Falaba Issa, 13
Traoré, Mahama Johnson, 15, 16, 17, 20, 22, 24
Traoré, Mory, 18
Tribal Scars, 113
Truffaut, François, 52, 79

UNESCO, 24
Union Générale Cinématographique (UGC), 22
Upper Volta, 14, 23, 24

Vauthier, René, 6
Victoire en Chantant, La, 8
Vieyra, Paulin Soumanou, 10, 13, 17, 20, 77
Vodio, N'Dabian, 15
Voltaïque, 113, 118
Voyage au Congo, 6

Wamba, 14
Wazou du Polygame, Le, 13
Welles, Orson, 56
Wolof: as film language, 25, 99, 114, 127, 131, 133, 149, 157, 165; music, 66; as a people, 73, 120; symbolic use of, 57, 156

Xala, 149–63; censorship of, 46–47; characters in, 16, 34, 35, 51, 53, 55–56, 60–61; as comedy, 71, 72–73, 74; film technique in, 48–49, 50, 51, 52, 79; griot in, 32, 33; and history, 43; language of, 25; plot, 113; political concern in, 16–17; soundtrack, 64, 65–66, 68; and symbolism, 58–59, 69; and traditional theater, 38; viewers of, 21

Zaire, 10, 117
Zulu, 7

About the Author

FRANÇOISE PFAFF is Associate Professor of French at Howard University. She has published articles in *Positif, Commonwealth, Jump Cut, Black Art,* the *College Language Association Journal,* and elsewhere. She has also lectured on African film at French and American universities, the Smithsonian Institution, the National Museum of African Art, and the Institute for Policy Studies.